Captains' Legal

By: Captain Michael Lloyd, FNI

First edition published 2009

ISBN 978 - 1 - 905331 - 40 - 6

British Library Cataloguing in Publication Data
A catalogue record for this book is available from the British Library.

Notice of Terms of Use

While the advice given in this book Captains' Legal has been developed using the best information currently available, it is intended purely as guidance to be used at the user's own risk. Witherby Seamanship International Ltd accepts no responsibility for the accuracy of any information or advice given in the document or any omission from the document or for any consequence whatsoever resulting directly or indirectly from compliance with or adoption of guidance contained in the document even if caused by failure to exercise reasonable care.

This publication has been prepared to deal with the subject of the essential elements of maritime law. This should not, however, be taken to mean that this publication deals comprehensively with all of the issues that will need to be addressed or even, where a particular issue is addressed, that this publication sets out the only definitive view for all situations.

The opinions expressed are those of the author only and are not necessarily to be taken as the policies or views of any organisation with which he has any connection.

Printed and bound in Great Britain by Bell & Bain Ltd, Glasgow

Published in 2009 by

Witherby Seamanship International Ltd
4 Dunlop Square, Livingston
Edinburgh, EH54 8SB
Scotland, UK

Tel No: +44(0)1506 463 227
Fax No: +44(0)1506 468 999
Email: info@emailws.com
www.witherbyseamanship.com

Foreword

This is an excellent precis on Maritime Law to assist the Master.

Any Master should feel comfortable with, and better armed to deal with, most of the Maritime minefield he may encounter after reading it.

Captain Edward Martin Scott, RD, FNI, RNR**
Immediate Past Master of the Honourable Company of Master Mariners
January 2009

Author's Introduction

As we sail our ships around the world, we come into contact with various rules and regulations, some of which we are familiar with and others not, especially those applicable only to the country that the ship is visiting. However, maritime law is designed to be internationally applicable wherever a ship is and, in theory at least, is designed to deal with maritime incidents regardless of flag or administration.

How Well do you Know your Rules? Do you Find yourself Embroiled in Red Tape?

Many problems arise because one side or another does not understand the applicable law for a given event. Worse still, reliance is often placed, by the shore authorities, on the Masters of ships not knowing the applicable law at the time when it is in their interest to do so.

There are a number of books dealing with all aspects of maritime law and business and *'The Shipmaster's Business Companion'* by Malcolm Maclachlan is an excellent book for those wishing to delve further into maritime law, particularly for British vessels. However, the aim of this book is to explain, in plain language, the laws for incidents and problems that a Master might encounter on an average vessel, of any registration, while going about normal business on the seas and in the ports.

It is important to remember that often, with an incident, unless it is obvious who or what is to blame, everyone believes that they are right. A problem can only be solved within the context of the law, together with reason and a willingness to listen. Always remember that calmness and courtesy go a long way toward resolution. As

Master, your job is to resolve any matter in the best interests of your company, so you must at all times bear in mind that what you say and do will have an effect on the eventual outcome of any case.

In all incidents and events that may cause claims to be made against your vessel, your company or yourself, or in situations where you, on behalf of your company, might be making a claim against another party, maintenance of records is essential. These should be supported by photographs and witness statements. Often during an emergency, everyone is too fully occupied coping with the problems to write a log of events. However, if this is the case, as soon as possible after the event, the log must be written up while things are still fresh in everyone's minds.

If you are going to take a deliberate action that could have legal consequences for your owners/operators or charterers, where possible you must consult with them before taking this action. This does not display doubt on your part, but is a sensible approach to the legal minefield of maritime law that we know little about. Your operator is better positioned to call upon specialist legal assistance if it is appropriate to do so.

It would be pleasant to say that, if the law supports your case, everything should be fine. Unfortunately politics, both local and national, can come into play and cause various aspects of the law to be interpreted more freely than intended, or even put aside for the sake of expediency. There is a need in all of us for fair play or justice, but unfortunately justice is a concept that varies considerably in the various states that we visit. If the same legal thought that has gone into Charter Parties had gone into the treatment of seafarers, many of our current problems would have been resolved. However, we must deal with what exists rather than what could or should be. Regrettably, in a few cases, payment of some kind or other may be the only solution. There is a time to wave the books of law around and there are times to sit down and negotiate. The art is knowing the time and place to do either of these.

Tug Fees $1,250, Berthing Dues $3,000, Pilotage Fees $1,750, Garbage Fine $250. Catching the Last Tide Out...Priceless. There are Some Things Money Can Buy, For Everything Else There's a Shipmaster's Means of Persuasion

At the time of writing, there have been several high profile cases which illustrate the legal difficulties faced by seafarers, with two pollution related incidents of particular concern. The first involves the Master and Chief Officer of the *'Hebei Spirit'*, whose initial acquittal and subsequent imprisonment after appeal by the prosecution, allegedly on the back of national public opinion, have been widely condemned throughout the industry. The evidence in the Korean Maritime Safety Tribunal Interim Report was described by INTERTANKO Managing Director Peter Swift as "nonsensical and flawed", reflecting the opinions of a large proportion of the industry.

The second prominent case concerns the Master of the *'Prestige'*, who after being arrested in a "knee-jerk reaction by a flailing government" (ITF seafarers' secretary Jon Whitlow) was consequently detained for 83 days. After appealing against this detainment, a unanimous decision by the Strasbourg court ruled that the €3m bail was not excessive and the period spent in a Spanish jail was short compared with comparable cases. The fact that the coastal State's handling of the event contributed in making a manageable casualty into a major environmental incident does not appear to be considered significant.

Finally, an apology for all the laws and rules quoted. This is necessary if you are to have a reference to quote from when appropriate to the occasion. I have tried to deal only with the sections that have relevance to us as Masters as we sail around the world under a host of different flags, subject to their regulations and reliant on their support. The problem with maritime law is that its international nature makes it more complex than national law, and it is written by lawyers for lawyers rather than for seafarers. We need the Law of the Sea, but what we need now is for it to be followed by the States that agreed to it in the first place.

Captain Michael Lloyd, RD**, FNI, RNR (Rtd)
Younger Brother of Trinity House
Member of the Honourable Company of Master Mariners
Senior Advisor, Witherby Seamanship International Ltd

Acknowledgements

UN Convention on the Law of the Sea

IMO Resolution A.871 (20) – 'Guidelines on the Allocation of Responsibilities to Seek the Successful Resolution of Stowaway Cases'

IMO Resolution A.989 (24) – 'Guidelines on the Fair Treatment of Seafarers in the Event of a Maritime Accident'

IMO Resolution A.949 (23) – 'Guidelines on Places of Refuge for Ships in Need of Assistance'

Maritime Coastguard Agency

Royal Navy

Evia (No. 2) [1983] 1 AC 736 at 757

Eastern City [1958] 2LL Rep 127 at 131, approved by the House of Lords in the Evia at 749 and 756

SS Knutsford Ltd v Tillmanns & Co [1908] 2 KB 385 (CA), [1908] AC 406 (HL) and the 'Hermine' [1979] 1 Lloyd's Rep 212

Ogden v Graham (1861) 1 B&S 773; Reardon Smith Line v Australian Wheat Board [1956] AC 266; Evans v Bullock 91877038 LT 34

Julian Morgan of Morgans

Captain Donal Linehan, FNI

International Transport Federation - www.ITFGLOBAL.org

International Labour Organization - www.ILO.org

International Maritime Organization - www.IMO.org

Steamship Mutual

Seaways article 'Fair Treatment of Seafarers' by Captain Laxlo Kovats

Contents

Foreword **iii**

Author's Introduction **v**

Acknowledgements **ix**

1 Who Owns the Seas? **1**
1.1 The High Seas 3
1.2 Illegal Narcotics 5
1.3 Terrorism 7
1.4 Boarding Provisions 8
1.5 Passage through Straits 13
1.6 Contiguous Zone 15
1.7 Exclusive Economic Zone 16
1.8 Continental Shelf 17
1.9 Internal Waters 17

2 Criminal Jurisdiction **19**
2.1 Civil Jurisdiction in Relation to Foreign Ships 24

3 The Flag State **25**
3.1 Duties of the Flag State 25
3.2 Flag State Penal Jurisdiction 27

4 Pollution **29**
4.1 The Rights of the State 31
4.2 Sewage 39
4.3 Prevention of Pollution by Garbage from Ships 39
4.4 Garbage Management Plans 43
4.5 The Investigation of Ships 43
4.6 The Ship's Rights 44

5 Stowaways **47**
5.1 Stowaway Onboard 50
5.2 The State of Embarkation 54
5.3 The Flag State 54
5.4 Inadequate Documentation 55

6 Port of Refuge **57**
6.1 Towing and Salvage 60
6.2 Act of Voluntary Salvage 60
6.3 Towage 60
6.4 Tow or Salvage 61
6.5 Pollution Compensation 62

7 Charterers and Charter Parties **63**
7.1 The Voyage Charter 63
7.2 The Time Charter 63
7.3 Bareboat Charters 64
7.4 Charter Party Disputes 64
7.5 Affreightment 65
7.6 Bill of Lading 65
7.7 Mate's Receipt 66

7.8 Deadfreight 67
7.9 Safe Port 67
7.10 Laytime 68
7.11 Demurrage 68
7.12 Notice of Readiness (NOR) 68
7.13 On-Hire, Off-Hire 67
7.14 Cargo Stowage 70
7.15 Stevedore Damage 71
7.16 Protest 71

8 Insurance 73
8.1 P&I Clubs 73
8.2 General Average 75

9 Ballast Water Management 77

10 Operating in Ice 81

11 Ocean Routeing 85

12 Refugees 87
12.1 The Ship is not a Place of Safety 88

13 Mutiny 91
13.1 A Recent Act of Mutiny? 92

14 The Fair Treatment of Seafarers (After a Maritime Accident) 95
14.1 Flag State 98
14.2 The Seafarer's State 99
14.3 The Shipowner 100
14.4 The Seafarer 100

15 Shore Leave and Seafarers' Rights 105
15.1 Seafarers' Rights Onboard 106
15.2 Legal Assistance for Seafarers 107

16 Manning and Fatigue 109

17 Port State Control 113
17.1 Areas Where the Port State Control Operates 113
17.2 The Inspectors 114
17.3 Targeting Ships 114
17.4 The White List 115
17.5 The Grey List 115
17.6 The Black List 115
17.7 Inspections 115
17.8 Types of Inspections 116
17.9 Detention 117
17.10 Safeguards 117

18 The Law in Inland Waters 119
18.1 The Arrest of Ships 120
18.2 The Powers of Arrest 121
18.3 Release from Arrest 121
18.4 The ISPS Code 122

19 Conclusion 123

1 Who Owns the Seas?

Approximately 70% of the Earth's Surface is Covered by Water

You would think that, with having to spend most of our working lives on the seas, we would know something about who owns and controls the parts we sail through. Many of us do not. However, with controls over the seas increasing, it is important that we should know at least the basics of the Laws of the Seas and the areas to which they refer.

The control of various parts of the seas has become increasingly difficult to define as, over the years, more and more zones have been declared.

The UN Convention on the Law of the Sea, commonly referred to as UNCLOS, set the zones of coastal State jurisdiction and the High Seas.

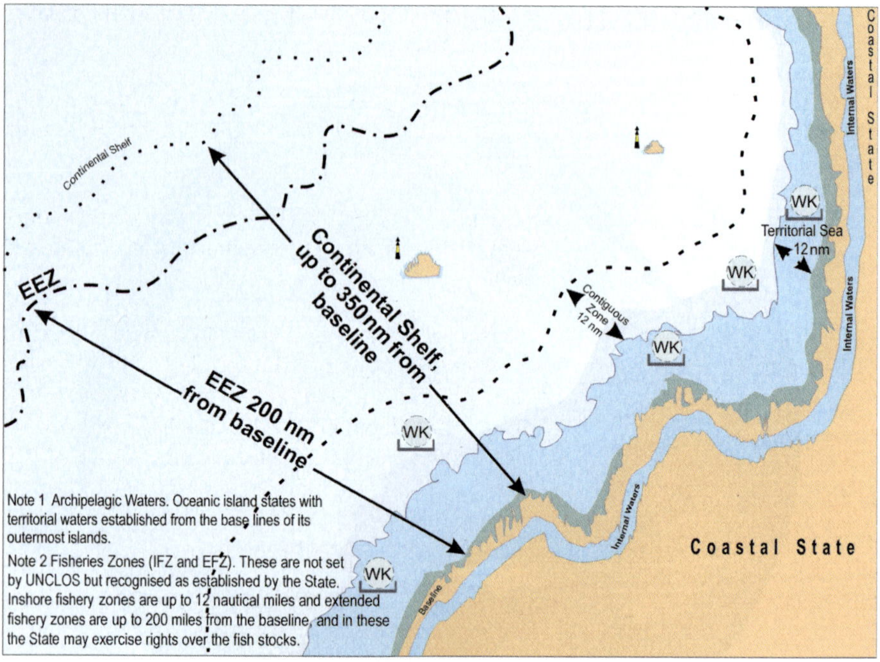

UNCLOS Limits

Internal Waters

These are the waters between the shore and the baseline.

Baseline

The normal baseline is the low water line along the coast, as marked on the charts and officially recognised by the coastal State. If there are offshore islands or reefs then the baseline may be extended to them.

Territorial Sea

This typically extends 12 nautical miles from the baseline.

The High Seas

Water beyond the jurisdiction of any State.

Contiguous Zone

Can extend 12 nautical miles beyond the Territorial Sea limit.

Exclusive Economic Zone (EEZ)	Can extend to a maximum of 200 nautical miles from the baseline.
Continental Shelf	This is a 'resource zone' only, with no territorial rights. It may extend up to 350 nautical miles from the baseline.
Archipelagic Waters	Oceanic island States with territorial waters established from the baselines of its outermost islands.
Fisheries Zones (IFZ and EFZ)	These are not set by UNCLOS but are recognised as established by the State. Inshore fishery zones are up to 12 nautical miles from the baseline and extended fishery zones are up to 200 miles from the baseline, and in these the State may exercise rights over the fish stocks.

1.1 The High Seas

Article 87 is reproduced from UNCLOS of 10th December 1982.

UNCLOS is a 202 page document. A PDF is available at:
http://www.un.org/Depts/los/convention_agreements/texts/unclos/unclos_e.pdf

Article 87 of the Law of the Sea states:

1. The high seas are open to all States, whether coastal or land-locked. Freedom of the high seas is exercised under the conditions laid down by this Convention and by other rules of international law. It comprises, *inter alia*, both for coastal and land-locked States:

   (a) freedom of navigation;
   (b) freedom of overflight;
   (c) freedom to lay submarine cables and pipelines, subject to certain conditions;
   (d) freedom to construct artificial islands and other installations permitted under international law, subject to certain conditions;
   (e) freedom of fishing, subject to certain conditions;
   (f) freedom of scientific research, subject to certain conditions.

2. These freedoms shall be exercised by all States with due regard for the interests of other States in their exercise of the freedom of the high seas, and also with due regard for the rights under this Convention with respect to activities in the Area.

Article 87 does seem to define a right to free passage, without let or hinderance, except during time of war. So we can sail the seas, build islands and fish off them. However, Article 110 goes on to define a list of occasions when it is permissible to stop vessels on the high seas, called 'Right of Visit'.

Do you know when a Navy Team can Pay you a Visit?

3. Except where acts of interference derive from powers conferred by treaty, a warship which encounters on the high seas a foreign ship, other than a ship entitled to complete immunity in accordance with Articles 95 and 96, is not justified in boarding it unless there is reasonable ground for suspecting that:

   (a) the ship is engaged in piracy;
   (b) the ship is engaged in the slave trade;
   (c) the ship is engaged in unauthorized broadcasting and the Flag State of the warship has jurisdiction under Article 109;
   (d) the ship is without nationality; or
   (e) though flying a foreign flag or refusing to show its flag, the ship is, in reality, of the same nationality as the warship.

4. In the cases provided for in paragraph 1, the warship may proceed to verify the ship's right to fly its flag. To this end, it may send a boat under the command of an officer to the suspected ship. If suspicion remains after the documents have been checked, it may proceed to a further examination onboard the ship, which must be carried out with all possible consideration.

5. If the suspicions prove to be unfounded, and provided that the ship boarded has not committed any act justifying them, it shall be compensated for any loss or damage that may have been sustained.

6. These provisions apply to military aircraft.
7. These provisions also apply to any other duly authorized ships or aircraft clearly marked and identifiable as being on government service.

The boarding of merchant ships is an act normally observed in support of UN sanctions against certain countries. A case where you would need to know your rights could occur in Asia, where pirates have operated naval looking vessels (wearing suitable uniforms) and have stopped merchant ships under naval pretences. While claiming otherwise, their motive has been theft of personal effects or cargo or the ship itself, with no respect for the ship's crew.

1.2 Illegal Narcotics

The present 'Rights of Visit' allowed on the high seas seem to prohibit warships or Government vessels from boarding ships suspected of illegal narcotic trafficking or engagement in terrorist activities. However, there is an ambiguity as the law states there must be 'reasonable grounds for suspecting'. What are reasonable grounds? If, for example, a vessel is approached by a warship that states that they suspect the vessel of engaging in piracy and wish to visit, how does the vessel know the grounds the warship is acting on? Is that the real reason why the visit is requested or could there be other reasons? If during that visit they find a crew member in possession of illegal narcotics in his cabin, without the knowledge of the Master, what is the position? By law, they can take no action against the ship, the Master or the crew member.

Another set of laws to examine is the The UN Vienna Convention of 1988, which is occasionally quoted in the 'war on drugs'.

Taken from the UN Convention against the Illicit Traffic in Narcotic Drugs and Psychotropic Substances, 1988

Article 17 states:

1. The Parties shall co-operate to the fullest extent possible to suppress illicit traffic by sea, in conformity with the international law of the sea.
2. A Party which has reasonable grounds to suspect that a vessel flying its flag or not displaying a flag or marks of registry is engaged in illicit traffic may request the assistance of other Parties in suppressing its use for that purpose. The Parties so requested shall render such assistance within the means available to them.
3. A Party which has reasonable grounds to suspect that a vessel exercising freedom of navigation in accordance with international law and flying the flag or displaying marks of registry of another Party is engaged in illicit traffic may so notify the Flag State, request confirmation of registry and, if confirmed, request authorization from the Flag State to take appropriate measures in regard to that vessel.

4. In accordance with paragraph 3 or in accordance with treaties in force between them or in accordance with any agreement or arrangement otherwise reached between those Parties, the Flag State may authorize the requesting State to, *inter alia*:

   (a) board the vessel;
   (b) search the vessel;
   (c) if evidence of involvement in illicit traffic is found, take appropriate action with respect to the vessel, persons and cargo onboard.

However, in conforming to the international law of the sea as stated in section 1, such an action would not be allowed on the high seas except where the laws of hot pursuit were applicable.

5. Where action is taken pursuant to this article, the Parties concerned shall take due account of the need not to endanger the safety of life at sea, the security of the vessel and the cargo or to prejudice the commercial and legal interests of the Flag State or any other interested State.

This is interesting as the mere act of detaining a vessel does interfere with the commercial interests of the ship, especially when such a delay causes a vessel to miss a berth. Provided that no illegal narcotics are found, who then compensates the owners or operators for such costs, the party who requested the action or the Flag State that took it?

6. The Flag State may, consistent with its obligations in paragraph 1 of this article, subject its authorization to conditions to be mutually agreed between it and the requesting Party, including conditions relating to responsibility.

7. For the purposes of paragraphs 3 and 4 of this article, a Party shall respond expeditiously to a request from another Party to determine whether a vessel that is flying its flag is entitled to do so, and to requests for authorization made pursuant to paragraph 3. At the time of becoming a Party to this Convention, each Party shall designate an authority or, when necessary, authorities to receive and respond to such requests. Such designation shall be notified through the Secretary-General to all other Parties within one month of the designation.

8. A Party which has taken any action in accordance with this article shall promptly inform the Flag State concerned of the results of that action.

9. The Parties shall consider entering into bilateral or regional agreements or arrangements to carry out, or to enhance the effectiveness of, the provisions of this article.

10. Action pursuant to paragraph 4 of this article shall be carried out only by warships or military aircraft, or other ships or aircraft clearly marked and identifiable as being on government service and authorized to that effect.

11. Any action taken in accordance with this article shall take due account of the need not to interfere with or affect the rights and obligations and the exercise of jurisdiction of coastal States in accordance with the international law of the sea.

As with all of these articles, we see once again that, according to paragraph 1, the law of the sea takes precedence.

To finish this section, Article 108 of the Law of the Sea states:

1. All States shall cooperate in the suppression of illicit traffic in narcotic drugs and psychotropic substances engaged in by ships on the high seas contrary to international conventions.
2. Any State which has reasonable grounds for believing that a ship flying its flag is engaged in illicit traffic in narcotic drugs or psychotropic substances may request the cooperation of other States to suppress such traffic.

Therefore, your own Flag State, in fulfilling its cooperative agreements, can request a visitation from another State's warship or Government vessel. Of course, any warship wishing to board a vessel that refuses to comply will be instantly in contact with the Flag State for their authority. Once that is granted, visitation can legally take place.

1.3 Terrorism

The Law of the Sea does not mention acts of a terrorist nature. However, the '2005 Protocol to the SUA Convention' published as an amendment to the 'IMO Convention for the Suppression of Unlawful Acts against the Safety of Maritime Navigation 1988' added a new Article 3bis, which states that:

A person commits an offence within the meaning of the Convention if that person unlawfully and intentionally:

- when the purpose of the act, by its nature or context, is to intimidate a population, or to compel a Government or an international organization to do or to abstain from any act;
- uses against or on a ship or discharging from a ship any explosive, radioactive material or BCN (biological, chemical, nuclear) weapon in a manner that causes or is likely to cause death or serious injury or damage;
- discharges, from a ship, oil, liquefied natural gas, or other hazardous or noxious substance, in such quantity or concentration that causes or is likely to cause death or serious injury or damage;
- uses a ship in a manner that causes death or serious injury or damage;

What is interesting here is that, should the Master, officer or helmsman be intoxicated or under the influence of any narcotics when an accident on the vessel leads to death, damage or injury, could the fact that they intentionally took such substances be construed as a deliberate act? What about crew members in a similar state engaged in a bunkering incident leading to pollution?

The transportation of nuclear material is not considered an offence if such item or material is transported to or from the territory of, or is otherwise transported under the control of, a State Party to the Treaty on the Non-Proliferation of Nuclear Weapons (subject to conditions).

Under the new instrument, a person commits an offence within the meaning of the Convention if that person unlawfully and intentionally transports another person onboard a ship knowing that the person has committed an act that constitutes an offence under the SUA Convention or an offence set forth in any treaty listed in the Annex. The Annex lists nine such treaties.

The new instrument also makes it an offence to unlawfully and intentionally injure or kill any person in connection with the commission of any of the offences in the Convention; to attempt to commit an offence; to participate as an accomplice; to organise or direct others to commit an offence; or to contribute to the commissioning of an offence.

It must be noted that these laws only apply where any person or persons have deliberately committed an offence or participated in one. The act of participation is also clarified by the word 'accomplice'. In other words, even if a crew member committed any offence listed, the Master and officers are innocent provided that they did not know about or participate in the action.

1.4 Boarding Provisions

Taken from the UN Convention for the Suppression of Unlawful Acts Against the Safety of Maritime Navigation, 1988

Article 8 of the SUA Convention covers the responsibilities and roles of the Master of the ship, Flag State and receiving State in delivering to the authorities of any State Party any person believed to have committed an offence under the Convention, including the furnishing of evidence pertaining to the alleged offence.

A new Article 8bis in the 2005 Protocol covers co-operation and procedures to be followed if a State Party desires to board a ship flying the flag of a State Party when the requesting Party has reasonable grounds to suspect that the ship or a person onboard the ship is, has been, or is about to be involved in, the commission of an offence under the Convention.

The authorization and co-operation of the Flag State is required before such a boarding. A State Party may notify the IMO Secretary-General that it would allow authorization to board and search a ship flying its flag, its cargo and persons onboard if there is no response from the Flag State within four hours, commonly referred to as the Silence Period. A State Party can also notify that it authorizes a requesting Party to board and search the ship, its cargo and persons onboard, and to question the persons onboard to determine if an offence has been, or is about to be, committed.

This tells us that lack of response from your Flag State to a request to board your vessel by another State authorises the boarding. Once boarded, both ship and personnel can be searched and questioned.

The use of force is to be avoided except when necessary to ensure the safety of officials and persons onboard, or where the officials are obstructed in the execution of authorised actions.

This means that reasonable force is permitted to ensure the safety of those boarding, under the rather dubious grounds of being 'obstructed' in their actions. Is refusal to answer questions considered grounds for force or for the forcible removal of a person from the ship? What is the position of the Master if he allows the removal of a person from his ship when the law of the sea requires him to protect the safety of everyone under his command, especially if the Master is not shown any reason for that removal?

Article 8bis includes important safeguards when a State Party takes measures against a ship, including boarding. The safeguards include: not endangering the safety of life at sea; ensuring that all persons onboard are treated in a manner which preserves human dignity and in keeping with human rights law; taking due account of safety and security of the ship and its cargo; ensuring that measures taken are environmentally sound; and making reasonable efforts to avoid a ship being unduly detained or delayed.

As most of us are not engaged in piracy, the slave trade or other heinous acts, we should continue to be free from any stopping and boarding. We can see that it is important to display your flag during daylight when approached by any warship or Government auxiliary vessel, such as coastguard craft. Anyone boarding must be under the command of an officer.

Raise your Flag in the Presence of Naval Ships

The most sensible action would seem to be that, on the approach of any warship or Government vessel on the high seas, you ensure that your flag is clearly displayed by day and at night and you clearly identify your vessel on the VHF. If you are requested to stop, you are entitled to know why. This would also seem to be an appropriate time to contact your Designated Person Ashore (DPA) and advise him of the situation. He should contact your Flag State on your behalf to advise them of the stopping and ask if they have given their authority for this or for any form of visitation. At this stage, a request might be made to allow a visit. If you agree, then a visit may go ahead on the basis of the Master's authority to board, although you do not have to grant this. If you are concerned about the proper identity or authority of the visiting vessel, you should advise them that you are waiting for authority from your Flag State.

Taken from UNCLOS

Article 2, Territorial Waters

1. The sovereignty of a coastal State extends, beyond its land territory and internal waters and, in the case of an archipelagic State, its archipelagic waters, to an adjacent belt of sea, described as the territorial sea.
2. This sovereignty extends to the air space over the territorial sea as well as to its bed and subsoil.
3. The sovereignty over the territorial sea is exercised subject to this Convention and to other rules of international law.

Article 3

Every State has the right to establish the breadth of its territorial sea up to a limit not exceeding 12 nautical miles, measured from baselines determined in accordance with this Convention.

Article 12

Roadsteads, which are normally used for the loading, unloading and anchoring of ships, and which would otherwise be situated wholly or partly outside the outer limit of the territorial sea, are included in the territorial sea.

Article 17

Subject to this Convention, ships of all States, whether coastal or land-locked, enjoy the right of innocent passage through the territorial sea.

What to note here is that, although the territorial rights only extend to 12 nautical miles from the baseline, in circumstances where there are offshore terminals or anchorages belonging to that Flag State, and regardless of the fact that they are more than 12 nautical miles from their baseline, these waters are still considered to be within that State's territorial waters for the purposes of the Laws of the Sea and so are subject to the laws and restrictions of that State's territorial waters.

Article 18

1. 'Passage' means navigation through the territorial sea for the purpose of:
   (a) traversing that sea without entering internal waters or calling at a roadstead or port facility outside internal waters; or
   (b) proceeding to or from internal waters or a call at such roadstead or port facility.
2. Passage shall be continuous and expeditious. However, passage includes stopping and anchoring, but only in so far as the same are incidental to ordinary navigation or are rendered necessary by *force majeure* or distress or for the purpose of rendering assistance to persons, ships or aircraft in danger or distress.

Article 19

1. Passage is innocent so long as it is not prejudicial to the peace, good order or security of the coastal State. Such passage shall take place in conformity with this Convention and with other rules of international law.
2. Passage of a foreign ship shall be considered to be prejudicial to the peace, good order or security of the coastal State if in the territorial sea it engages in any of the following activities:
   (a) any threat or use of force against the sovereignty, territorial integrity or political independence of the coastal State, or in any other manner in violation of the principles of international law embodied in the Charter of the United Nations;
   (b) any exercise or practice with weapons of any kind;

(c) any act aimed at collecting information to the prejudice of the defence or security of the coastal State;
(d) any act of propaganda aimed at affecting the defence or security of the coastal State;
(e) the launching, landing or taking onboard of any aircraft;
(f) the launching, landing or taking onboard of any military device;
(g) the loading or unloading of any commodity, currency or person contrary to the customs, fiscal, immigration or sanitary laws and regulations of the coastal State;
(h) any act of wilful and serious pollution contrary to this Convention;
(i) any fishing activities;
(j) the carrying out of research or survey activities;
(k) any act aimed at interfering with any systems of communication or any other facilities or installations of the coastal State;
(l) any other activity not having a direct bearing on passage.

This means that, provided your ship is on innocent passage through a State's waters and not stopping for the odd barbeque on a nice beach, you have a right of passage. Anchoring for repairs and assisting those in distress does not interfere with your rights.

The coastal State through whose waters you must pass is allowed to adopt laws and regulations which, provided that they conform with the provisions of the Law of the Sea and other international rules, relate to innocent passage.

These laws and regulations will concern:

Taken from UNCLOS

(a) the safety of navigation and the regulation of maritime traffic;
(b) the protection of navigational aids and facilities and other facilities or installations;
(c) the protection of cables and pipelines;
(d) the conservation of the living resources of the sea;
(e) the prevention of infringement of the fisheries laws and regulations of the coastal State;
(f) the preservation of the environment of the coastal State and the prevention, reduction and control of pollution thereof;
(g) marine scientific research and hydrographic surveys;
(h) the prevention of infringement of the customs, fiscal, immigration or sanitary laws and regulations of the coastal State.

It is the responsibility of the coastal State to publicise all such laws and regulations. However, ignorance of the law is not allowed as a defence.

The laws go on to state that any such laws and rules adopted by a State should not apply to the design, construction or manning of foreign ships in its waters unless they interfere with the vessel's ability to conform to generally accepted rules or standards. This opens the door to deal with situations where a ship is thought not to be capable of safely transiting the waters.

Once these laws are made and disseminated, it is the duty of all foreign ships exercising the right of innocent passage to comply with them, in addition to complying with international regulations relating to prevention of collision at sea.

If the rules and laws are complied with, the coastal State must not hamper the innocent passage of foreign ships. In particular, it should not impose requirements on foreign ships that are designed to hamper them. An example of this would be where the State required something that ships could not conform to, such as displaying a large red balloon or painting the ship white!

In addition, they should not discriminate against the ships of any State or against ships carrying cargoes to, from or on behalf of any State.

1.5 Passage through Straits

With the many changes in territorial waters and exclusive economic zones, many straits that previously were part of the high seas are now under the control of one State. The Law of the Sea that covers this circumstance is as follows:

Taken from UNCLOS Article 38 Rights of Transit Passage

1. In straits referred to in article 37, all ships and aircraft enjoy the right of transit passage, which shall not be impeded; except that, if the strait is formed by an island of a State bordering the strait and its mainland, transit passage shall not apply if there exists seaward of the island a route through the high seas or through an exclusive economic zone of similar convenience with respect to navigational and hydrographical characteristics.

I must admit that, in the past, when transiting the Sunda Strait with time on my hands, I have done a little sightseeing around Krakatoa to the North. Under these rules, I did not have right of passage. It is interesting to speculate on how cruise vessels, which frequently make such diversions from the high seas or economic zones to take their passengers sightseeing, view compliance with this article.

2. Transit passage means the exercise in accordance with this Part of the freedom of navigation and overflight solely for the purpose of continuous and expeditious transit of the strait between one part of the high seas or an exclusive economic zone and another part of the high seas or an exclusive economic zone. However, the requirement of continuous and expeditious transit does not preclude passage through the strait for the purpose of entering, leaving or returning from a State bordering the strait, subject to the conditions of entry to that State.

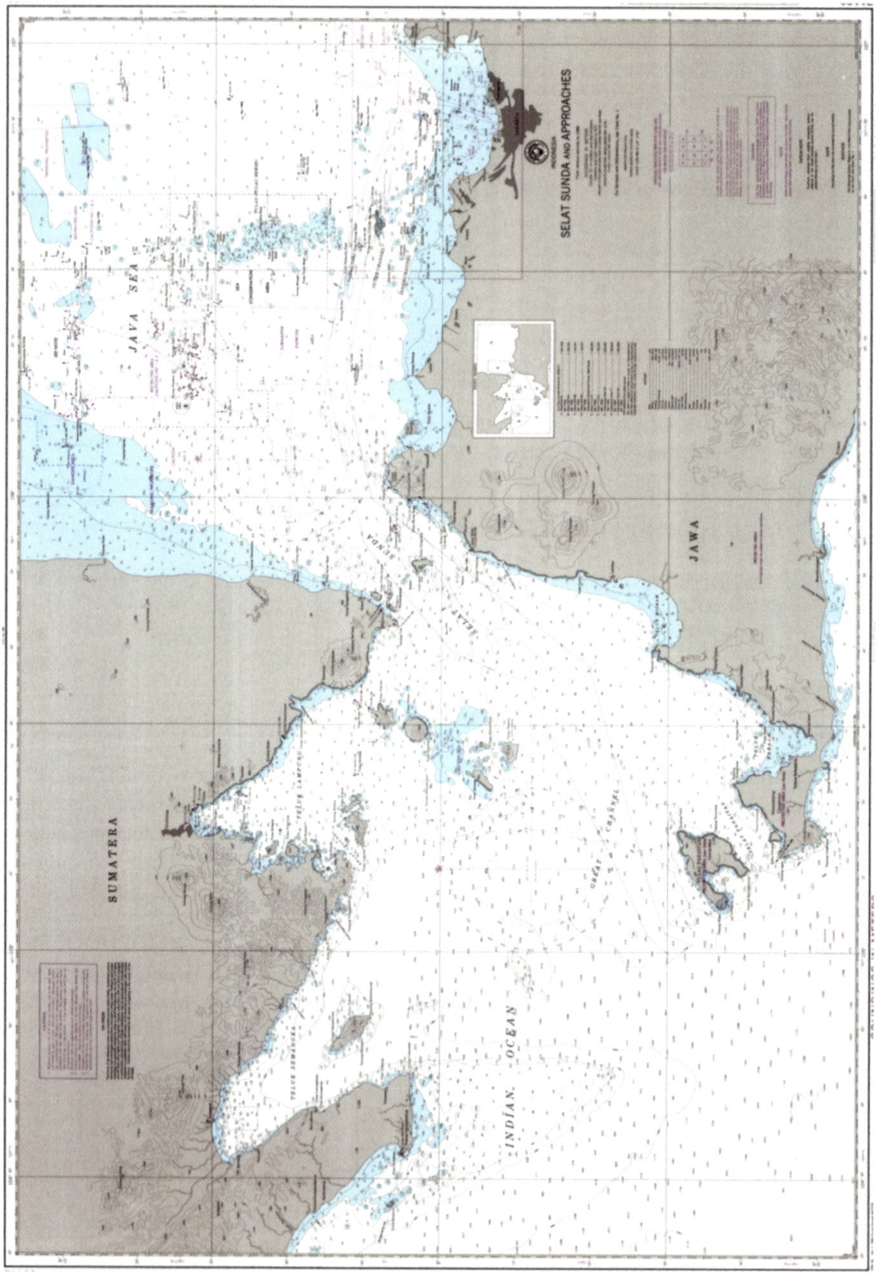

Sunda Strait is One of the Many Straits Around the World that Offers Ships the Right of Transit Passage

3. Any activity which is not an exercise of the right of transit passage through a strait remains subject to the other applicable provisions of this Convention.

While ships are in transit of these passages, they shall:

Article 39

1. (a) proceed without delay through or over the strait;
   (b) refrain from any threat or use of force against the sovereignty, territorial integrity or political independence of States bordering the strait, or in any other manner in violation of the principles of international law embodied in the Charter of the United Nations;
   (c) refrain from any activities other than those incident to their normal modes of continuous and expeditious transit unless rendered necessary by *force majeure* or by distress;

2. (a) comply with generally accepted international regulations, procedures and practices for safety at sea, including the *International Regulations for Preventing Collisions at Sea*;
   (b) comply with generally accepted international regulations, procedures and practices for the prevention, reduction and control of pollution from ships.

The states bordering such straits may enact laws and regulations relating to the ships exercising their rights of passage through these waters concerning the following:

Article 42

1. (a) the safety of navigation and the regulation of maritime traffic;
   (b) the prevention, reduction and control of pollution, by giving effect to applicable international regulations regarding the discharge of oil, oily wastes and other noxious substances in the strait;
   (c) with respect to fishing vessels, the prevention of fishing, including the stowage of fishing gear;
   (d) the loading or unloading of any commodity, currency or person in contravention of the customs, fiscal, immigration or sanitary laws and regulations of States bordering straits.

In other words, the same responsibilities and restrictions apply to vessels transiting the coastal States within the straits as in territorial or exclusive economic zones.

1.6 Contiguous Zone

Taken from UNCLOS

Article 33

1. In a zone contiguous to its territorial sea, described as the contiguous zone, the coastal State may exercise the control necessary to:

   (a) prevent infringement of its customs, fiscal, immigration or sanitary laws and regulations within its territory or territorial sea;

(b) punish infringement of the above laws and regulations committed within its territory or territorial sea.

2. The contiguous zone may not extend beyond 24 nautical miles from the baselines from which the breadth of the territorial sea is measured.*

* Note. The Democratic People's Republic of Korea declared a 50 nautical mile military zone. Army Command Announcement of 1st August 1977.

This effectively creates a barrier of waters between the high seas and a State's territorial waters. Within, it can interdict a vessel that it has **reasonable** grounds to suspect of breaking its laws. Note that, if a vessel is proved to have broken the laws, it can be detained and punishments imposed.

Vessels, or vessels carrying cargoes, that are perceived as dangerous to a State could, under the sanitary laws and on the grounds of public health, be turned away if necessary. Therefore, ships looking for a port of refuge could be refused entry into waters up to 24 nautical miles away. The same laws can also be used for pollution, again under the sanitation provision.

Taken from UNCLOS

1.7 Exclusive Economic Zone

In the exclusive economic zone, the coastal State has:

Article 56

1. (a) sovereign rights for the purpose of exploring and exploiting, conserving and managing the natural resources, whether living or non-living, of the waters superjacent to the seabed and of the seabed and its subsoil, and with regard to other activities for the economic exploitation and exploration of the zone, such as the production of energy from the water, currents and winds;

   (b) jurisdiction as provided for in the relevant provisions of this Convention with regard to:

      (i) the establishment and use of artificial islands, installations and structures;

      (ii) marine scientific research;

      (iii) the protection and preservation of the marine environment;

   (c) other rights and duties provided for in this Convention.

This can extend for up to 200 nautical miles away from a State's baseline and refers to the State's rights over natural resources within the zone.

All ships have the freedom of navigation enjoyed on the high seas in this zone, but with the proviso that the States have the right to restrict navigation near offshore installations.

In October 2008, Britain presented a formal claim to the United Nations for the seabed within a 350 mile radius of Ascension Island in the South Atlantic. As you will have seen with regard to EEZ limits, Britain can assert territorial rights to the area 200 nautical miles from the baseline. Under the terms of UNCLOS, this distance can be extended if the country in question can show that the continental shelf extends significantly into the ocean. If this claim is recognised, it will pave the way for exploration of a further 77,000 square miles of the Atlantic seabed around Ascension. While the waters around Ascension may not possess much in the way of oil and gas reserves, this claim could be a trial run for a British attempt to secure sovereignty over the contentious waters around the Falkland Islands, which are almost certainly rich in oil and gas deposits.

1.8 Continental Shelf

This is a resource zone and does not affect your right of passage. The waters in the zone are 'high seas'.

Article 76

1. The continental shelf of a coastal State comprises the seabed and subsoil of the submarine areas that extend beyond its territorial sea throughout the natural prolongation of its land territory to the outer edge of the continental margin, or to a distance of 200 nautical miles from the baselines from which the breadth of the territorial sea is measured where the outer edge of the continental margin does not extend up to that distance.

This shelf should not extend more than 350 miles from the baseline.

The rights of a State over the continental shelf are for the purpose of exploration and exploitation of natural resources, not including fish.

1.9 Internal Waters

The waters on the landward side of the baseline of the territorial sea form part of the internal waters of the State.

A State has complete jurisdiction over all internal waters. Innocent rights of passage are not allowed.

2 Criminal Jurisdiction

When can Criminal Jurisdiction be Exercised by a Coastal State?

In Chapter 1, we established the areas of responsibility over navigable waters by States and ships in transit, as defined in the Law of the Sea. This chapter examines the right of criminal jurisdiction by States over ships and those onboard, and the areas such jurisdiction can extend to. We will also look at the rights of the ships calling on States for assistance when in their jurisdiction.

Taken from UNCLOS

The Law of the Sea states:

Article 27

1. The criminal jurisdiction of the coastal State should not be exercised onboard a foreign ship passing through the territorial sea to arrest any person or to conduct any investigation in connection with any crime committed onboard the ship during its passage, save only in the following cases:

    (a) if the consequences of the crime extend to the coastal State;
    (b) if the crime is of a kind to disturb the peace of the country or the good order of the territorial sea;

(c) if the assistance of the local authorities has been requested by the master of the ship or by a diplomatic agent or consular officer of the Flag State; or
(d) if such measures are necessary for the suppression of illicit traffic in narcotic drugs or psychotropic substances.

This deals with territorial waters, but it must be remembered that, while these extend to 12 nautical miles from the baseline, the contiguous zone extends to 24 nautical miles. This means that (a), (b) and (d) can extend through the contiguous zone on the basis that the crimes are against the State's customs, fiscal, immigration or sanitary regulations, whereas (c) provides a law that assists the Master in dealing with a problem on his ship when it is in a State's territorial waters. As this law is of criminal jurisdiction, it would only apply to matters of a criminal nature. This means that, for example, the Master could call for assistance in dealing with criminal acts by crew or passengers. However, it also means that, if he suspects the carriage of narcotics, it could be investigated by the coastal State.

Taken from UNCLOS

2. The part 1 provisions do not affect the right of the coastal State to take any steps authorized by its laws for the purpose of an arrest or investigation onboard a foreign ship passing through the territorial sea after leaving internal waters.

Do you know when a State can Dispatch a Warship in Pursuit of a Merchant Vessel?

If the State suspects that the ship or a person onboard has violated its laws, the act of sailing from that port is only a navigational act and so does not free the ship or the person from the jurisdiction of that State. Even if the act took place while sailing through the territorial waters or the contiguous zone, the State has the right of 'hot pursuit'. This expression means that the State may authorise a clearly marked warship, or other ship or aircraft belonging to a Government agency, to pursue a ship and board, even on the high seas, exactly as if the ship was still in its territorial waters. However, there is a distinction as to which laws and rules the ship can be pursued for. In internal waters, any act that is deemed by the State as breaking its laws and rules will apply. If the ship is on passage in territorial waters then 'hot pursuit' can only be undertaken when it is suspected that the rules and regulations applicable to territorial waters have been violated. If the ship is transiting the contiguous zone, only when it is suspected of transgressing the contiguous laws and rules of the State can pursuit be undertaken.

Taken from UNCLOS Article 111

The laws on 'hot pursuit' are as follows:

1. The hot pursuit of a foreign ship may be undertaken when the competent authorities of the coastal State have good reason to believe that the ship has violated the laws and regulations of that State. Such pursuit must be commenced when the foreign ship or one of its boats is within the internal waters, the archipelagic waters, the territorial sea or the contiguous zone of the pursuing State, and may only be continued outside the territorial sea or the contiguous zone if the pursuit has not been interrupted. It is not necessary that, at the time when the foreign ship within the territorial sea or the contiguous zone receives the order to stop, the ship giving the order should likewise be within the territorial sea or the contiguous zone. If the foreign ship is within a contiguous zone, the pursuit may only be undertaken if there has been a violation of the rights for the protection of which the zone was established.

2. The right of hot pursuit shall apply *mutatis mutandis* (i.e. when the necessary changes have been made) to violations in the exclusive economic zone or on the continental shelf, including safety zones around continental shelf installations, of the laws and regulations of the coastal State applicable in accordance with this Convention to the exclusive economic zone or the continental shelf, including such safety zones.

3. The right of hot pursuit ceases as soon as the ship pursued enters the territorial sea of its own State or of a third State.

4. Hot pursuit is not deemed to have begun unless the pursuing ship has satisfied itself by such practicable means as may be available that the ship pursued or one of its boats or other craft working as a team and using the ship pursued as a mother ship is within the limits of the territorial sea, or, as the case may be, within the contiguous zone or the exclusive economic zone or above

the continental shelf. The pursuit may only be commenced after a visual or auditory signal to stop has been given at a distance which enables it to be seen or heard by the foreign ship.

Can a Warship Literally Fire a Shot Across your Bows?

The distance at which a vessel must be warned to stop is important. The pursuing vessel must initially be within a visual or auditory signal. From this, we can assume that VHF or radar distance is not sufficient, on the basis that an auditory signal is that of a ship's whistle, siren or gun. Hot pursuit cannot be initiated by a shore based traffic control or coastguard service. It must commence with the physical presence of a vessel that is within the zones specified.

5. The right of hot pursuit may be exercised only by warships or military aircraft, or other ships or aircraft clearly marked and identifiable as being on government service and authorized to that effect.

6. Where hot pursuit is effected by an aircraft:

    (a) the provisions of paragraphs 1 to 4 shall apply;
    (b) the aircraft giving the order to stop must itself actively pursue the ship until a ship or another aircraft of the coastal State, summoned by the aircraft,

arrives to take over the pursuit, unless the aircraft is itself able to arrest the ship. It does not suffice to justify an arrest outside the territorial sea that the ship was merely sighted by the aircraft as an offender or suspected offender, if it was not both ordered to stop and pursued by the aircraft itself or other aircraft or ships which continue the pursuit without interruption.

7. The release of a ship arrested within the jurisdiction of a State and escorted to a port of that State for the purposes of an inquiry before the competent authorities may not be claimed solely on the ground that the ship, in the course of its voyage, was escorted across a portion of the exclusive economic zone or the high seas, if the circumstances rendered this necessary.

8. Where a ship has been stopped or arrested outside the territorial sea in circumstances which do not justify the exercise of the right of hot pursuit, it shall be compensated for any loss or damage that may have been thereby sustained.

Of course, in the process of hot pursuit, there is no way that the Master can know if it is legal. If a suspected offence under territorial waters rules did not start until the ship was clear of territorial waters and in the contiguous zone, who is going to tell him? In this, we are entirely dependant on the State following the laws and, unfortunately, there are States that are not too particular in this regard. Aircraft are not easily identifiable from a ship's decks, exacerbating the issue. Unfortunately, there is no provision that says communications have to be established with the suspect vessel at the outset, which if implemented would save confusion on both sides. I once experienced hot pursuit as a young officer while on patrol with the Royal Navy in Northern Ireland. The vessel refused to stop and it was pursued into international waters with the pursuit being transferred to aircraft and then to another vessel. The ship was eventually escorted into a UK port for inspection.

Taken from UNCLOS Article 27

3. In the cases provided for in paragraphs 1 and 2, the coastal State shall, if the master so requests, notify a diplomatic agent or consular officer of the Flag State before taking any steps, and shall facilitate contact between such agent or officer and the ship's crew. In cases of emergency this notification may be communicated while the measures are being taken.

In shipping, as in life, there are few moments as grave as those when you are asked if you want your lawyer present. Refer to the next chapter on Flag State duties and responsibilities.

4. In considering whether or in what manner an arrest should be made, the local authorities shall have due regard to the interests of navigation.

5. Except as provided in Part XII (which deals with the protection and preservation of the marine environment) or with respect to violations of laws and regulations adopted in accordance with Part V (which outlines the restrictions within the

exclusive economic zone) the coastal State may not take any steps onboard a foreign ship passing through the territorial sea to arrest any person or to conduct any investigation in connection with any crime committed before the ship entered the territorial sea, if the ship, proceeding from a foreign port, is only passing through the territorial sea without entering internal waters.

2.1 Civil Jurisdiction in Relation to Foreign Ships

Taken from UNCLOS Article 28

1. The coastal State should not stop or divert a foreign ship passing through the territorial sea for the purpose of exercising civil jurisdiction in relation to a person onboard the ship.
2. The coastal State may not levy execution against or arrest the ship for the purpose of any civil proceedings, save only in respect of obligations or liabilities assumed or incurred by the ship itself in the course or for the purpose of its voyage through the waters of the coastal State.
3. Paragraph 2 is without prejudice to the right of the coastal State, in accordance with its laws, to levy execution against or to arrest, for the purpose of any civil proceedings, a foreign ship lying in the territorial sea, or passing through the territorial sea after leaving internal waters.

This is extremely important as it protects the rights of those onboard a ship that is exercising its rights of innocent passage. It means that no arrests or detentions can take place unless the ship has committed an offence against the laws applicable to the State zones that the ship passes through.

3 The Flag State

Some Flags have rather Stringent Registration Conditions, while others are Exceptionally Lenient

Throughout the various laws and convention resolutions, references are frequently made to the responsibilities of the Flag State. It is therefore necessary that the Master should have an understanding of the responsibilities of the Flag State as well as his obligations under these statutes.

With regard to your Flag, the Law of the Sea states:

Taken from UNCLOS Article 91

1. Every State shall fix the conditions for the grant of its nationality to ships, for the registration of ships in its territory, and for the right to fly its flag. Ships have the nationality of the State whose flag they are entitled to fly. There must exist a genuine link between the State and the ship.
2. Every State shall issue to ships to which it has granted the right to fly its flag documents to that effect

I am sure that there are a few smiles at the rather free interpretation of the terms 'genuine link' that we see from many ships and companies.

3.1 Duties of the Flag State

Taken from UNCLOS Article 94

The Law of the Sea states:

1. Every State shall effectively exercise its jurisdiction and control in administrative, technical and social matters over ships flying its flag.

2. In particular every State shall:

   (a) maintain a register of ships containing the names and particulars of ships flying its flag, except those which are excluded from generally accepted international regulations on account of their small size; and
   (b) assume jurisdiction under its internal law over each ship flying its flag and its Master, officers and crew in respect of administrative, technical and social matters concerning the ship.

3. Every State shall take such measures for ships flying its flag as are necessary to ensure safety at sea with regard, *inter alia*, to:

   (a) the construction, equipment and seaworthiness of ships;
   (b) the manning of ships, labour conditions and the training of crews, taking into account the applicable international instruments;
   (c) the use of signals, the maintenance of communications and the prevention of collisions.

4. Such measures shall include those necessary to ensure:

   (a) that each ship, before registration and thereafter at appropriate intervals, is surveyed by a qualified surveyor of ships, and has onboard such charts, nautical publications and navigational equipment and instruments as are appropriate for the safe navigation of the ship;
   (b) that each ship is in the charge of a master and officers who possess appropriate qualifications, in particular in seamanship, navigation, communications and marine engineering, and that the crew is appropriate in qualification and numbers for the type, size, machinery and equipment of the ship;
   (c) that the Master, officers and, to the extent appropriate, the crew are fully conversant with and required to observe the applicable international regulations concerning the safety of life at sea, the prevention of collisions, the prevention, reduction and control of marine pollution, and the maintenance of communications by radio.

5. In taking the measures called for in paragraphs 3 and 4 each State is required to conform to generally accepted international regulations, procedures and practices and to take any steps which may be necessary to secure their observance.

6. A State which has clear grounds to believe that proper jurisdiction and control with respect to a ship have not been exercised may report the facts to the Flag State. Upon receiving such a report, the Flag State shall investigate the matter and, if appropriate, take any action necessary to remedy the situation.

7. Each State shall cause an inquiry to be held by or before a suitably qualified person or persons into every marine casualty or incident of navigation on the high seas involving a ship flying its flag and causing loss of life or serious injury to nationals of another State or serious damage to ships or installations of another State or to the marine environment. The Flag State and the other State shall cooperate in the conduct of any inquiry held by that other State into any such marine casualty or incident of navigation.

The majority of this is known to seafarers through the annual Flag State inspections. These ensure that the standards required by the Flag State are observed onboard the vessel. However, there are a few sections that deserve closer study.

Paragraph 2b, which states the Flag State's jurisdiction on the vessel under its own internal law, gives rise to the requirement that vessels carry a copy of that State's maritime law to ensure compliance. For good management of the ship, it is prudent to have an understanding of the State's laws, especially where they differ from the norm.

Kangaroo court

A kangaroo court or kangaroo trial, sometimes likened to a drumhead court-martial or drumhead trial, is a sham legal proceeding or court. Kangaroo courts are judicial proceedings that deny due process in the name of expediency. The outcome of such a trial is essentially made in advance, usually for the purpose of providing a conviction, either by going through the motions of manipulated procedure or by allowing no defence at all.

Paragraph 7 is also of special interest as it means that, in any incident on the high seas, only your Flag State can hold an inquiry into your conduct, regardless of the other States involved. However, it also states that, while your Flag State must cooperate with their inquiries, the onus of the investigation into your ship and actions remains with your Flag State.

3.2 Flag State Penal Jurisdiction

Taken from UNCLOS Article 97

1. In the event of a collision or any other incident of navigation concerning a ship on the high seas, involving the penal or disciplinary responsibility of the master or of any other person in the service of the ship, no penal or disciplinary proceedings may be instituted against such person except before the judicial or administrative authorities either of the Flag State or of the State of which such person is a national.
2. In disciplinary matters, the State which has issued a Master's certificate or a certificate of competence or licence shall alone be competent, after due legal process, to pronounce the withdrawal of such certificates, even if the holder is not a national of the State which issued them.
3. No arrest or detention of the ship, even as a measure of investigation, shall be ordered by any authorities other than those of the Flag State.

This is very important as it means that any investigation or disciplinary measures taken against the ship or any person on that ship, over any navigational incident, can only be carried out by its Flag State and that there can be no arrest or detention of the ship for an incident except by order of the Flag State.

The statements could not be more clear. However, the following shows the extent of the regard some States have for the Law of the Sea.

The Cypriot flag vessel *'Virgo'*, with a Russian crew, was allegedly involved in a collision with a US fishing vessel, involving loss of life on the fishing vessel, in international waters 130 miles off the US coast. The vessel was arrested in Newfoundland and held in a Canadian port at the request of the US Government, in complete contravention of the Flag State laws. The crew were ordered off the vessel at gunpoint and the Master was imprisoned by the Canadian authorities, together with the OOW and the lookout. The Master was eventually released but detained in Canada for a further 18 months, ultimately released against a US$100,000 bond while extradition charges were pending.

The Transport Ministry demanded explanations as to why the inquiry was being conducted by the Canadian authorities. In line with the United Nations' Maritime Law Convention, the investigation should have been carried out by the authorities of the State whose flag the ship flew, i.e. the Cypriot flag.

It was alleged that both the US and Canada had violated the UN Law of the Sea Convention by initiating criminal proceedings in this case.

It was argued that the US-Canadian investigation was in breach of the UN Maritime Convention. Russia formally complained to Ottawa that Canadian police had illegally removed the crew of the *'Virgo'* during a search of the vessel.

Cypriot shipping authorities also challenged the legality of a joint US-Canadian criminal investigation.

As a contrasting example, in 1991 three Indian crew members from the Cypriot flagged *'Zulfikar'* were tried in Cyprus after their ship collided with a trawler off Portsmouth in the English Channel in an accident that claimed the lives of several fishermen. The UK Government fully complied with the law.

4 Pollution

***'Torrey Canyon'* (Getty)**

In 1967, the tanker *'Torrey Canyon'* ran aground while entering the English Channel, spilling a total cargo of 120,000 tons of crude oil into the sea. This was the biggest oil pollution incident that had ever been recorded up to that time.

The incident showed how inadequate the oil pollution regulations were and exposed the problems with compensation. It prompted the IMO to call an extraordinary session of the Council and, in 1969, agreement was reached to hold an international conference in 1973 that would deal with contamination of the sea, land and air by ships. To ratify this agreement, 15 nations totalling over 50% of the world merchant tonnage had to sign it, but this did not happen. However, in 1978, following a number of accidents at sea involving further large scale pollution, the IMO held another Conference that resulted in the adoption of the MARPOL convention on 17th February 1978.

The standard reference book is *MARPOL, Annex 1*, which contains the regulations for the prevention of pollution by oil. It lists all the special areas where mandatory regulation is required and the regulations for all other areas. Rather than list all of these here, it is enough to say that the discharge of any oil at sea is prohibited unless certain criteria, that can be found in MARPOL, are met.

MARPOL Regulation 4

Under Regulation 4 of MARPOL, Annex I, there are certain exceptional circumstances where the discharge of oil is acceptable. These are:

1. The discharge into the sea of oil or oily mixture necessary for the purpose of securing the safety of a ship or saving life at sea; or
2. The discharge into the sea of oil or oily mixture resulting from damage to a ship or its equipment:
    1. Provided that all reasonable precautions were taken after the occurrence of the damage or discovery of the discharge for the purpose of preventing or minimising the discharge; and
    2. Except if the Owner or Master acted either with intent to cause damage, or recklessly and with knowledge that damage would probably result; or
    3. Discharge into the sea of substances containing oil approved by the Administration, when being used for the purpose of combating specific pollution incidents in order to minimise the damage from pollution. Any such discharge will be subject to the approval of any Government in whose jurisdiction it is contemplated this discharge will occur.

GO TO JAIL, DO NOT PASS GO, DO NOT COLLECT £200.
In the unfortunate event of a pollution incident, you'll hope you have a 'get out of jail free' card!

The last clauses are important as, in the event of any damage caused to the ship or equipment by fire, explosion, grounding or collision, we are not subject to prosecution under any pollution regulations provided that we can show that everything possible was done to contain any discharge. The use of chemicals in this prevention is severely restricted to those that contain no oil, unless approval is given by the Government that holds jurisdiction over the waters where the incident occurred. This should apply to any chemicals you intend to use.

Pollution has become an emotive and political issue, generating a large number of regulations. Because of political and media pressure, States need to be seen to be acting when there is any major pollution incident. In any pollution case, especially in controlled waters, a State has certain rights.

4.1 The Rights of the State

Taken from the International Federation of Shipmasters' Associations draft guidelines to the IMO conference regarding the fair treatment of seafarers in the event of a maritime accident

Taken from UNCLOS Article 211

1. States, acting through the competent international organization or general diplomatic conference, shall establish international rules and standards to prevent, reduce and control pollution of the marine environment from vessels and promote the adoption, in the same manner, wherever appropriate, of routeing systems designed to minimize the threat of accidents which might cause pollution of the marine environment, including the coastline, and pollution damage to the related interests of coastal States. Such rules and standards shall, in the same manner, be re-examined from time to time as necessary.

Any coastal State, in areas where it has control of navigation, can therefore order routeing as required on the grounds of pollution and vessels transiting such areas have to follow this routeing.

2. States shall adopt laws and regulations for the prevention, reduction and control of pollution of the marine environment from vessels flying their flag or of their registry. Such laws and regulations shall at least have the same effect as that of generally accepted international rules and standards established through the competent international organization or general diplomatic conference.

All Flag States now have to adopt the minimum pollution prevention controls required by MARPOL. Any State can, of course, add to these requirements.

3. States which establish particular requirements for the prevention, reduction and control of pollution of the marine environment as a condition for the entry of foreign vessels into their ports or internal waters or for a call at their off-shore terminals shall give due publicity to such requirements and shall communicate them to the competent international organization. Whenever such requirements are established in identical form by two or more coastal States in an endeavour to harmonize policy, the communication shall indicate which States are participating in such cooperative arrangements. Every State shall require the Master of a vessel flying its flag or of its registry, when navigating within the territorial sea of a State participating in such cooperative arrangements, to furnish, upon the request of that State, information as to whether it is proceeding to a State of the same region participating in such cooperative arrangements and, if so, to indicate whether it complies with the port entry requirements of that State. This article is without prejudice to the continued exercise by a vessel of its right of innocent passage or to the application of Article 25, paragraph 2.

The problem with this is, while your actions might conform to the particular regulations of one State, the next port State you visit could have a different set of regulations that you are expected to comply with.

4. Coastal States may, in the exercise of their sovereignty within their territorial sea, adopt laws and regulations for the prevention, reduction and control of marine pollution from foreign vessels, including vessels exercising the right of innocent passage. Such laws and regulations shall, in accordance with Part II, section 3, not hamper innocent passage of foreign vessels.

This means that, whatever rules the coastal State imposes within territorial waters to control pollution, they should not hamper the passage of transiting ships.

5. Coastal States, for the purpose of enforcement as provided for in section 6, may in respect of their exclusive economic zones adopt laws and regulations for the prevention, reduction and control of pollution from vessels conforming to and giving effect to generally accepted international rules and standards established through the competent international organization or general diplomatic conference.

6. (a) Where the international rules and standards referred to in paragraph 1 are inadequate to meet special circumstances and coastal States have reasonable grounds for believing that a particular, clearly defined area of their respective exclusive economic zones is an area where the adoption of special mandatory measures for the prevention of pollution from vessels is required for recognized technical reasons in relation to its oceanographical and ecological conditions, as well as its utilization or the protection of its resources and the particular character of its traffic, the coastal States, after appropriate consultations through the competent international organization

with any other States concerned, may, for that area, direct a communication to that organization, submitting scientific and technical evidence in support and information on necessary reception facilities. Within 12 months after receiving such a communication, the organization shall determine whether the conditions in that area correspond to the requirements set out above. If the organization so determines, the coastal States may, for that area, adopt laws and regulations for the prevention, reduction and control of pollution from vessels implementing such international rules and standards or navigational practices as are made applicable, through the organization, for special areas. These laws and regulations shall not become applicable to foreign vessels until 15 months after the submission of the communication to the organization.

Coastal States can Protect Areas of Outstanding Beauty or Define Certain 'no-go' Areas

This means that, if a State wishes to set up a designated marine park off its coast or designate a particular reef area as endangered, or wants to ensure that strict rules are in place regarding pollution, this regulation allows for those new restrictions to be imposed once the defined area had been approved and adequate time interval has been allowed for the information to be provided to vessels.

(b) The coastal States shall publish the limits of any such particular, clearly defined area.

(c) If the coastal States intend to adopt additional laws and regulations for the same area for the prevention, reduction and control of pollution from vessels, they shall, when submitting the aforesaid communication, at the same time notify the organization thereof. Such additional laws and regulations may relate to discharges or navigational practices but shall not require foreign vessels to observe design, construction, manning or equipment standards other than generally accepted international rules and standards; they shall become applicable to foreign vessels 15 months after the submission of the communication to the organization, provided that the organization agrees within 12 months after the submission of the communication.

The economic zone extends to 200 nautical miles beyond the baseline so areas that have permission granted within this zone can have specific rules that do not generally apply to the State's economic zone. However, it could be argued that the fishing zones of a State can also be included as any pollution would affect the environment within those zones.

7. The international rules and standards referred to in this article should include *inter alia* those relating to prompt notification to coastal States, whose coastline or related interests may be affected by incidents, including maritime casualties, which involve discharges or probability of discharges

None of this seems unreasonable. When you are within a State's controlled waters, over which it has legal rights regarding pollution, you must follow the laws of that State provided that they do not conflict with international law. In respect of navigation, provided that the information has been provided to ships by the state, the State can direct ships to route away from sensitive areas and, if within territorial waters, the State has control of the navigation of ships under the Law of the Sea.

To ensure that ships comply with the regulations made by the State, various enforcement laws are allowed. These are as follows;

Taken from UNCLOS Article 217

1. States shall ensure compliance by vessels flying their flag or of their registry with applicable international rules and standards, established through the competent international organization or general diplomatic conference, and with their laws and regulations adopted in accordance with this Convention for the prevention, reduction and control of pollution of the marine environment from vessels and shall accordingly adopt laws and regulations and take other measures necessary for their implementation. Flag States shall provide for the effective enforcement of such rules, standards, laws and regulations, irrespective of where a violation occurs.

2. States shall, in particular, take appropriate measures in order to ensure that vessels flying their flag or of their registry are prohibited from sailing, until they can proceed to sea in compliance with the requirements of the international rules and standards referred to in paragraph 1, including requirements in respect of design, construction, equipment and manning of vessels.

While the design and construction do not change for most vessels, the standard certificates issued by Class will continue to apply. The equipment is dealt with by a vessel's compliance with the SOLAS regulations. All of these requirements are governed by Class and international regulation, but manning is not. The ship carries a manning certificate issued by maritime authorities based on the word of the owner or operator. Should any accident occur and it can be determined that the ship was not adequately manned for the task undertaken when the accident occurred, there would be a case for litigation. There is a question whether the Master is also liable for the under-manning of his vessel.

3. States shall ensure that vessels flying their flag or of their registry carry onboard certificates required by and issued pursuant to international rules and standards referred to in paragraph 1. States shall ensure that vessels flying their flag are periodically inspected in order to verify that such certificates are in conformity with the actual condition of the vessels. These certificates shall be accepted by other States as evidence of the condition of the vessels and shall be regarded as having the same force as certificates issued by them, unless there are clear grounds for believing that the condition of the vessel does not correspond substantially with the particulars of the certificates.

4. If a vessel commits a violation of rules and standards established through the competent international organization or general diplomatic conference, the Flag State, without prejudice to articles 218, 220 and 228, shall provide for immediate investigation and where appropriate institute proceedings in respect of the alleged violation irrespective of where the violation occurred or where the pollution caused by such violation has occurred or has been spotted.

5. Flag States conducting an investigation of the violation may request the assistance of any other State whose cooperation could be useful in clarifying the circumstances of the case. States shall endeavour to meet appropriate requests of Flag States.

6. States shall, at the written request of any State, investigate any violation alleged to have been committed by vessels flying their flag. If satisfied that sufficient evidence is available to enable proceedings to be brought in respect of the alleged violation, Flag States shall without delay institute such proceedings in accordance with their laws.

7. Flag States shall promptly inform the requesting State and the competent international organization of the action taken and its outcome. Such information shall be available to all States.

8. Penalties provided for by the laws and regulations of States for vessels flying their flag shall be adequate in severity to discourage violations wherever they occur.

Once again, the Flag State is responsible for ensuring that the ship is up to the required international standard for sailing the seas and we are familiar enough with the inspection processes. The important parts of these laws refer to the investigation of any act of violation of the pollution rules. You will note that it is the responsibility of the Flag State to investigate any act of violation, wherever it occurs. The Flag State can call on other states involved for their cooperation in any such investigation.

However, when a vessel is in a port or offshore terminal of a State, that State has the authority to investigate any suspected act of pollution by the vessel, outside waters under its control, as per article 218:

1. When a vessel is voluntarily within a port or at an off-shore terminal of a State, that State may undertake investigations and, where the evidence so warrants, institute proceedings in respect of any discharge from that vessel outside the internal waters, territorial sea or exclusive economic zone of that State in violation of applicable international rules and standards established through the competent international organization or general diplomatic conference.

Have you Considered the Ultimate Powers Port State Inspectors may have?

If, during the course of a voyage, a ship has violated the pollution regulations of another State in that State's internal waters, territorial waters or exclusive economic zone then that State, the Flag State or any other State damaged by that violation can request proceedings to be instituted. The Flag State can request an investigation into pollution violations at any time that the ship is within a port or offshore terminal, irrespective of where it occurred.

A most important provision allowed for here is that a State can take measures to stop a ship from sailing if, during the course of any inspection of any vessel, it is considered that the vessel is in violation of international rules and regulations regarding seaworthiness in such a way that it might cause damage to the environment. It may permit the ship to sail to the nearest repair yard. On completion of repairs to the State's satisfaction, the ship must be allowed to resume her voyage immediately. So, even if no pollution has actually been caused, if it is considered that because of the situation on your ship pollution *might* occur, your ship can be detained until the situation is rectified.

The moral of this is to always ensure that your pollution equipment, procedures and maintenance are in good order, regardless of whether or not you are bunkering or engaging in any act that might cause pollution.

The areas and powers of the coastal State, with respect to pollution, are laid down in Article 220 of UNCLOS as follows:

1. When a vessel is voluntarily within a port or at an off-shore terminal of a State, that State may, subject to section 7, institute proceedings in respect of any violation of its laws and regulations adopted in accordance with this Convention or applicable international rules and standards for the prevention, reduction and control of pollution from vessels when the violation has occurred within the territorial sea or the exclusive economic zone of that State.

2. Where there are clear grounds for believing that a vessel navigating in the territorial sea of a State has, during its passage therein, violated laws and regulations of that State adopted in accordance with this Convention or applicable international rules and standards for the prevention, reduction and control of pollution from vessels, that State, without prejudice to the application of the relevant provisions of Part II, section 3, (which refers to innocent passage in the territorial sea) may undertake physical inspection of the vessel relating to the violation and may, where the evidence so warrants, institute proceedings, including detention of the vessel, in accordance with its laws, subject to the provisions of section 7.

3. Where there are clear grounds for believing that a vessel navigating in the exclusive economic zone or the territorial sea of a State has, in the exclusive economic zone, committed a violation of applicable international rules and standards for the prevention, reduction and control of pollution from vessels or laws and regulations of that State conforming and giving effect to such rules and standards, that State may require the vessel to give information regarding its identity and

port of registry, its last and its next port of call and other relevant information required to establish whether a violation has occurred.

4. States shall adopt laws and regulations and take other measures so that vessels flying their flag comply with requests for information pursuant to paragraph 3.

5. Where there are clear grounds for believing that a vessel navigating in the exclusive economic zone or the territorial sea of a State has, in the exclusive economic zone, committed a violation referred to in paragraph 3 resulting in a substantial discharge causing or threatening significant pollution of the marine environment, that State may undertake physical inspection of the vessel for matters relating to the violation if the vessel has refused to give information or if the information supplied by the vessel is manifestly at variance with the evident factual situation and if the circumstances of the case justify such inspection.

6. Where there is clear objective evidence that a vessel navigating in the exclusive economic zone or the territorial sea of a State has, in the exclusive economic zone, committed a violation referred to in paragraph 3 resulting in a discharge causing major damage or threat of major damage to the coastline or related interests of the coastal State, or to any resources of its territorial sea or exclusive economic zone, that State may, subject to section 7, (which refers to the high seas) provided that the evidence so warrants, institute proceedings, including detention of the vessel, in accordance with its laws.

7. Notwithstanding the provisions of paragraph 6, whenever appropriate procedures have been established, either through the competent international organization or as otherwise agreed, whereby compliance with requirements for bonding or other appropriate financial security has been assured, the coastal State if bound by such procedures shall allow the vessel to proceed.

This all means that, in the internal waters or offshore facilities of a State, a ship can be investigated for any suspected violation of the pollution rules and, if necessary, be detained.

It also means that, in the territorial waters of a State, provided that the State has clear grounds for suspecting any violation, the ship can be inspected and, if required, detained.

If there are clear grounds for suspecting that there has been a violation in the exclusive economic zone, whether navigating in that zone or the territorial waters of the State, a ship can be asked to provide information regarding that violation. If the State is not happy with the answers it gets, it may inspect that vessel. If clear evidence is found that pollution occurred, it may commence proceedings against the vessel, including detention. If a vessel is detained but appropriate financial guarantees are made or shown to be in place, the State detaining the vessel, if bound by the procedures, must release it.

However, the boundaries do not necessarily stop within these waters. Article 221 of UNCLOS provides a rather ambiguous law:

> Nothing in this Part shall prejudice the right of States, pursuant to international law, both customary and conventional, to take and enforce measures beyond the territorial sea proportionate to the actual or threatened damage to protect their coastline or related interests, including fishing, from pollution or threat of pollution following upon a maritime casualty or acts relating to such a casualty, which may reasonably be expected to result in major harmful consequences.

The difference between 'customary' and 'conventional' laws are known only to lawyers and are purely academic as far as we are concerned. The phrase 'taking measures beyond the territorial sea proportionate to the threat' is disturbing. How far beyond the territorial sea? Obviously this allows the State to include its fishing zones but does it allow rights into the high seas? What are proportionate measures? Bombing a ship? There are countries that might well consider that is a proportionate response to a potential major incident, hopefully after taking off the crew!

There is provision under Article 225 that any State exercising its rights over a foreign ship should not endanger its safe navigation. Presumably, this is to stop any close quarters situation developing, or a deliberate ramming when efforts are made to stop a vessel. If a ship is ordered into a port for investigation, the State must ensure that it is in a safe anchorage and that the marine environment is not exposed to any risk of pollution.

4.2 Sewage

International Convention for the Prevention of Pollution from Ships, 1973, as modified by the Protocol of 1978 relating thereto (MARPOL 73/78)

Sewage

> In the 2004 April amendments, the following applies:
>
> The revised Annex will apply to new ships engaged in international voyages, of 400 gross tonnage and above or which are certified to carry more than 15 persons. Existing ships will be required to comply with the provisions of the revised Annex IV five years after the date of its entry into force. The Annex requires ships to be equipped with either a sewage treatment plant or a sewage comminuting and disinfecting system or a sewage holding tank.
>
> The discharge of sewage into the sea will be prohibited, except when the ship has in operation an approved sewage treatment plant or is discharging comminuted and disinfected sewage using an approved system at a distance of more than three nautical miles from the nearest land; or is discharging sewage which is not comminuted or disinfected at a distance of more than 12 nautical miles from the nearest land.

4.3 Prevention of Pollution by Garbage from Ships

Garbage has also attracted the attention of environmentalists and politicians in recent years. A considerable amount has been blamed on ships but, while a proportion certainly does come from that source, far more comes from the land. However, it has been found that many of the items that were once discarded over the side without thought can cause severe problems because of the long process of degradation.

Floating Plastic Bag, or does it really look like a Jellyfish?

March 8, 2008 'The Times' - *Scientists and environmentalists have attacked a global campaign to ban plastic bags which they say is based on flawed science and exaggerated claims. The widely stated accusation that the bags kill 100,000 animals and a million seabirds every year are false, experts have told The Times. They pose only a minimal threat to most marine species, including seals, whales, dolphins and seabirds.*

Time taken for objects to dissolve at sea	
Paper bus ticket	2-4 weeks
Cotton cloth	1-5 months
Rope	3-14 months
Woollen cloth	1 year
Painted wood	13 years
Tin can	100 years
Aluminium can	200-500 years
Plastic bottle	450 years

Data source: Hellenic Marine Environment Protection Association (HELMEPA)
www.imo.org

The 1973 MARPOL Convention sought to eliminate and reduce the amount of garbage being dumped into the sea from ships.

Under Annex V of the Convention, garbage includes all kinds of food, domestic and operational waste, excluding fresh fish, that is generated during the normal operation of the vessel and is liable to be disposed of continuously or periodically.

Annex V totally prohibits the disposal of plastics anywhere into the sea and severely restricts discharge of other garbage from ships into coastal waters and 'special areas'.

The Annex also obliges Governments to ensure there are facilities at ports and terminals for the reception of garbage.

The 'special areas' established under the Annex are:

- the Mediterranean Sea
- the Baltic Sea
- the Black Sea
- the Red Sea
- the Gulfs
- the North Sea
- the Wider Caribbean Region
- the Antarctic.

All of these areas (except for the Antarctic) are subject to heavy traffic and their enclosed nature means they have a low water exchange.

Garbage Inspection has Become a Hot Topic

In a similar manner to amendments adopted by other MARPOL Annexes, the regulation makes it clear that port State control officers can inspect a foreign-flagged vessel '*where there are clear grounds for believing that the master or crew are not familiar with essential shipboard procedures relating to the prevention of pollution by garbage'* (MARPOL Annex I Regulation 11).

Implementation and enforcement was the additional focus of MARPOL Annex V Regulation 9, adopted in 1995, which required:

3. Every ship of 400 gross tonnage and above and every ship which is certified to carry 15 persons or more engaged in voyages to ports or offshore terminals under the jurisdiction of other Parties to the Convention and every fixed and floating platform engaged in exploration and exploitation of the sea-bed shall be provided with a Garbage Record Book. The Garbage Record Book, whether as a part of the ship's official log-book or otherwise, shall be in the form specified in the appendix to this Annex;

The date, time, position of ship, description of the garbage and the estimated amount incinerated or discharged must be logged and signed. The books must be kept for a period of two years after the date of the last entry. This regulation does not impose stricter requirements but it makes it easier to check that the regulations are being adhered to. (www.imo.org/environment)

Therefore, it is now essential that ships keep an accurate record of garbage dumping in order to prove innocence when any is sighted.

Regulation 9 came into force for:

- New ships from 1st July 1997. From 1st July 1998, all applicable ships built before 1st July 1997 also have to comply
- All ships of 400 gross tonnage and above
- Every ship certified to carry 15 persons or more
- Every fixed or floating platform engaged in exploration and exploitation of the seabed.

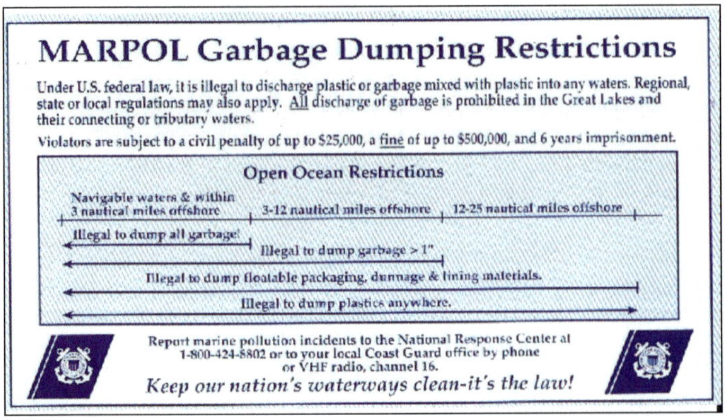

Garbage Disposal Placards are Required on all Vessels over 12 Metres in Length

The Regulation also requires every ship of 12 metres or more in length to display placards notifying passengers and crew of the disposal requirements of the Regulation. The placards should be in the official language of the ship's Flag State as well as in English or French for ships travelling to other States' ports or offshore terminals. (www.imo.org/environment)

4.4 Garbage Management Plans

Taken from MARPOL Annex V

All ships of 400 gross tonnage and above and every ship certified to carry 15 persons or more will have to carry a Garbage Management Plan, to include written procedures for collecting, storing, processing and disposing of garbage, including the use of equipment onboard. The Garbage Management Plan should designate the person responsible for carrying out the plan and should be in the working language of the crew.

4.5 The Investigation of Ships

Taken from UNCLOS Article 226

1. (a) States shall not delay a foreign vessel longer than is essential for purposes of the investigations provided for in articles 216, 218 and 220. Any physical inspection of a foreign vessel shall be limited to an examination of such certificates, records or other documents as the vessel is required to carry by generally accepted international rules and standards or of any similar documents which it is carrying; further physical inspection of the vessel may be undertaken only after such an examination and only when:

   (i) There are clear grounds for believing that the condition of the vessel or its equipment does not correspond substantially with the particulars of those documents;
   (ii) The contents of such documents are not sufficient to confirm or verify a suspected violation; or
   (iii) The vessel is not carrying valid certificates and records.

Provided that documents are in order, there must be clear grounds showing that the condition of the ship or equipment does not conform to that on the documents before any State inspection personnel can go round the ship, on deck or in the engine room, to inspect the equipment or for any other reason.

   (b) If the investigation indicates a violation of applicable laws and regulations or international rules and standards for the protection and preservation of the marine environment, release shall be made promptly subject to reasonable procedures such as bonding or other appropriate financial security.
   (c) Without prejudice to applicable international rules and standards relating to the seaworthiness of vessels, the release of a vessel may, whenever it would

present an unreasonable threat of damage to the marine environment, be refused or made conditional upon proceeding to the nearest appropriate repair yard.

This is fairly straightforward. If the State suspects violation and, while the case is pending, the owners or operators pay a bond or similar, then the State is required to let the vessel sail unless it considers that danger of pollution will continue to exist if the vessel sails. Permission can then be refused unless the vessel is sailing directly to a repair yard.

4.6 The Ship's Rights

Taken from UNCLOS Article 226

"States shall co-operate to develop procedures for the avoidance of unnecessary physical inspection of vessels at sea."

This is not a law, rather it is a statement of intent.

Taken from UNCLOS Article 227

The Law of the Sea states:

In exercising their rights and performing their duties under this Part, States shall not discriminate in form or in fact against vessels of any other State.

The idea behind this law is that, if there are political problems between two States, they should not affect the rights of innocent passage or the treatment of the ship while it is within the inland waters concerned.

Taken from Article 231

Notification to the Flag State and other States concerned.

States shall promptly notify the Flag State and any other State concerned of any measures taken pursuant to section 6 against foreign vessels, and shall submit to the Flag State all official reports concerning such measures. However, with respect to violations committed in the territorial sea, the foregoing obligations of the coastal State apply only to such measures as are taken in proceedings. The diplomatic agents or consular officers and where possible the maritime authority of the Flag State, shall be immediately informed of any such measures taken pursuant to section 6 against foreign vessels.

The following Laws are most important.

Taken from UNCLOS Article 292

1. Where the authorities of a State Party have detained a vessel flying the flag of another State Party and it is alleged that the detaining State has not complied with the provisions of this Convention for the prompt release of the vessel or its crew upon the posting of a reasonable bond or other financial security, the question of release from detention may be submitted to any court or tribunal agreed upon by the parties or, failing such agreement within 10 days from the time of detention, to a court or tribunal accepted by the detaining State under article 287 (Choice of Procedure) or to the International Tribunal for the Law of the Sea, unless the parties otherwise agree.
2. The application for release may be made only by or on behalf of the Flag State of the vessel.
3. The court or tribunal shall deal without delay with the application for release and shall deal only with the question of release, without prejudice to the merits of any case before the appropriate domestic forum against the vessel, its owner or its crew. The authorities of the detaining State remain competent to release the vessel or its crew at any time.
4. Upon the posting of the bond or other financial security determined by the court or tribunal, the authorities of the detaining State shall comply promptly with the decision of the court or tribunal concerning the release of the vessel or its crew.

This means that, if any ship or crew member has been detained, provided that suitable financial securities have been paid, it is up to the Flag State to request release. If the State holding the crew or ship does not comply with the release within 10 days of the case, without further delay, it must be placed before a court or tribunal agreed to by both sides. Once the financial securities posted are proved or determined by the court, the ship or crew members must be released.

If a State has not complied with the law for releasing a ship or the crew, the Flag State must make an application for it to go before a court.

There is an International Tribunal for the Law of the Sea and this is open to all State parties.

The coastal State is not allowed to stop or divert a foreign ship passing through its territorial waters to exercise civil jurisdiction over any person onboard, nor may it arrest the ship for any civil liabilities except in respect of any liabilities or obligations incurred during that ship's passage through its waters. The coastal State may arrest a ship for civil proceedings involving any incident that occurred during its time in internal waters.

5 Stowaways

Under the 2002 Amendment to the Convention of Facilitation of Maritime Traffic 1965, the following definitions apply:

A Stowaway 'is a person who is secreted on a ship or in cargo which is subsequently loaded on a ship, without the consent of the Ship-owner or the Master or any other responsible person and is detected onboard after the ship has sailed from a port and reported as a stowaway by the Master to the appropriate authorities'.

Stowaways are an increasing maritime problem that is no longer confined to the 'traditional' stowaway ports of the African continent. The costs of dealing with stowaways can be substantial, ranging from an average of US$20,000 to $40,000 up to $100,000, which does not include incidental costs such as charter party problems.

A stowaway arriving illegally in Hong Kong could be fined $3,000 or face up to three years in prison. The Master, owners and agents of the vessel could be fined up to $77,000 and imprisoned for up to seven years unless it can be proven that the crew took 'reasonable' steps to keep the stowaway from leaving the ship. The Chinese Government often seizes vessels, regardless of whether or not a Shipmaster is convicted.

In a past case, two Tanzanian stowaways stayed onboard a cargo ship for 315 days before they were repatriated.

The IMO statistics for the year 2006 showed 244 incidents involving 657 stowaways. Stowaways were found in:

Car decks (20)	Rudder trunks (5)
Containers (14)	Engine room (2)
Cargo holds (6)	Lifeboats (1)

and various storage and ventilation rooms around the ships.

The places with the highest risk were found to be:

Greece (overall) 91
Algiers, Algeria 43
Ostend, Belgium 23
Shanghai, People's Republic of China 22
Panama 7
Morocco (overall) 17
Istanbul, Turkey 14
Nigeria (overall) 9
South Africa 8

There were also 354 stowaways about which there is no information.

The ports with the highest numbers of attempted disembarkations were Venice, Italy and Ramsgate, UK.

The 2002 Amendment to the Convention of Facilitation of Maritime Traffic 1965 added a new section to the Convention stating:

> Public authorities, port authorities, ship-owners and their representatives and Shipmasters shall co-operate to the fullest extent possible in order to prevent stowaway incidents and to resolve stowaway cases expeditiously and secure that an early return or repatriation of the stowaway will take place. All appropriate measures shall be taken in order to avoid situations where stowaways must stay onboard ships indefinitely.

When stowaways are found onboard, all too often blame has been placed on the ship and the Master. However, the same new section requires that States implement in their ports the necessary infrastructure of operational and security arrangements to prevent anyone intent on stowing away from gaining access to the port installations and ships. This firmly fixes the prevention of stowaways as a shared responsibility between the port and the ship. It would be pleasant to think that, on arrival, the ship would be advised of the port stowaway prevention plan!

The 2002 Amendment to the Convention of Facilitation of Maritime Traffic 1965 states that the port should address the following:

- Regular patrol of port areas.
- Establishment of special storage areas for cargoes of high risk of access to stowaways and the monitoring of persons who have access to this facility.
- Inspections of warehouses and cargo areas.
- When the presence of stowaways is clearly indicated, a search of cargo itself.
- Co-operation between the port and the ship.
- Developing and instituting agreements with stevedores and other entities in the port to ensure that only personnel engaged in the cargo operations and other essential work participate in such operations.

- Developing and instituting agreements with companies providing such services that a list of personnel needing to board the ship is provided and that such personnel are easily identifiable.
- Encouraging the companies and personnel working in the port area to report anyone who is apparently not authorised to be there.

Some of this might come as a surprise to many at sea. Certainly I cannot remember ever being provided with a list of all of the stevedoring employees coming onboard in high risk ports.

The ship must have preventative measures in place to stop stowaways from boarding or to detect them prior to sailing.

It is essential that, apart from having security on your ship, all possible doors, lockers and any other places where it might be possible for stowaways to enter are well secured prior to entry.

The Best Measure is Still to Treat your Ship Like Fort Knox and Keep a Watchful Eye

The Convention recommends that the ship should take at least the following measures:

Taken from the 2002 Annex to the Convention of Facilitation of Maritime Traffic 1965

- All doors, hatches and means of access to holds and stores which are not used during the ship's stay should be kept locked.
- Access points to the ship should be kept to a minimum and be adequately secured.

- Areas seaward of the ship should be adequately secured.
- Adequate deck watch should be kept.
- Boarding and disembarking should where possible be tallied by the ship's crew, or after agreement with the Master, by others.
- Adequate means of communication should be maintained.
- At night, adequate means of lighting should be maintained, both inside and alongside the hull.

The problem with all this is the lack of manpower available to the ship and often the operator's reluctance to supplement it with shore labour.

Prior to sailing, time must be set aside for a thorough stowaway search that will require the participation of most of the ship's company.

In suspect ports, I suggest that, after a place is inspected, you put your own seal on it. This will indicate whether someone has entered in the time between the search and departure.

Remember that you are not allowed to use search methods that might harm the stowaway. Suggestions of flushing out with CS gas are definitely to be discouraged!

5.1 Stowaway Onboard

So you have sailed and, despite your precautions and searches, stowaways have got onboard and have been found or, as is more usually the case, they have handed themselves in.

There is an IMO Resolution, A.871 of 1997, on the allocation of responsibilities regarding stowaways, and it is important that the parts of this that have relevance to you are understood.

It must also be remembered that this Resolution established guidelines to be followed, not laws or regulations.

It is suggested that the following are your responsibilities:

- To make every effort to determine immediately the port of embarkation of the stowaway
- To make every effort to establish the identity, including the nationality, of the stowaway

- To prepare a statement containing all the information relevant to the stowaway ready for presentation to the appropriate authorities
- To notify the existence of the stowaway to the operators of the ship, the port of embarkation and the next port
- Not to depart from your planned route to seek the disembarkation of the stowaway unless it has been prearranged with the authorities at the intended disembarkation point.

Desert Islands are not there to be Populated by Stowaways

This means you do not just drop him off on some deserted island! There is a proviso to this effect in the 2002 amendment. This rule does not apply if there are extenuating security, health or compassionate reasons.

Taken from IMO Guidelines Relating to Stowaways

To ensure that the stowaway is presented at the next port of call to the authorities.

A very important rule to remember is that you must take the appropriate measures to ensure the security, general health, welfare and safety of the stowaway until he is disembarked.

This means that you must treat him humanely and provide him with bedding, soap and food, etc.

Considering security implications, any perceived threat by stowaways would require additional measures, eg bars on portholes and 'guards' posted.

If we assume you have complied with the provisions of the Resolution, the onus is on the next port, which is usually where the problem lies. The Resolution states

These are the pieces of information that should be collected as per the IMO Resolution A.871 (20) dated 27 November 1997 :-

1. SHIP DETAILS	**4. STOWAWAY DETAILS – IDENTIFICATION DOCUMENTS**
1.1 Name of Ship :	**4.1 ID document type**
1.2 IMO Number :	4.2 Passport No:
1.3 Flag :	4.3 When issued :
1.4 Company :	4.4 Where issued :
1.5 Company address :	4.5 Date of expiry :
1.6 Agent in next port :	4.6 Issued by :
1.7 Agent address :	**4.7 ID Card No :**
1.8 IRCS :	4.8 When issued :
1.9 Inmarsat Number :	4.9 Where issued :
1.10 Port of Registry :	4.10 Date of expiry :
1.11 Name of Master :	4.11 Issued by :
2. STOWAWAY DETAILS - TIMELINE	**4.12 Seaman's Book No :**
2.1 Place of Boarding	4.13 When issued
2.2 Date / time found on board :	4.14 Where issued
2.3 Country of boarding :	4.15 Date of expiry
2.4 Time spent in country of boarding :	**4.16 Emergency Passport No :**
2.5 Date/time of boarding :	4.17 When issued :
2.6 Intended port of destination :	4.18 Where issued :
2.7 Intended final destination (if different) :	4.19 Date of expiry :
2.8 Stated reasons for boarding the ship :	4.20 Issued by :
3. STOWAWAY DETAILS – PERSONAL DETAILS	**5. STOWAWAY DETAILS : PERSONAL CHARACTERISTICS**
3.1 Surname :	5.1 Height (cm) :
3.2 Given Name :	5.2 Weight (kg) :
3.3 Name by which known :	5.3 Complexion :
3.4 Religion :	5.4 Colour of eyes :
3.5 Gender :	5.5 Colour of hair :
3.6 Date of Birth :	5.6 Form of head/face :
3.7 Place of Birth :	5.7 Marks/characteristics :
3.8 Claimed nationality :	5.8 First language (spoken) :
3.9 Home address :	5.9 First language (read) :
3.10 Home town :	5.10 First language (written) :
3.11 Country of domicile :	5.11 Other languages (spoken) :
3.12 Profession(s) :	5.12 Other languages (read) :
3.13 Employer(s) names and addresses :	5.13 Other languages (written) :
3.14 Address in country of boarding :	**6. OTHER DETAILS :** Method of boarding, including other persons involved (e.g. crew, port workers etc) and whether they were secreted in cargo / container or hidden in the vessel :
3.15 Marital status :	
3.16 Name of spouse :	
3.17 Nationality of spouse :	
3.18 Address of spouse :	
3.19 Names of parents :	
3.20 Nationality of parents :	
3.21 Address of parents :	

7. OTHER DETAILS : Inventory of the stowaway's possessions :

8. OTHER DETAILS : Was the stowaway assisted in boarding the vessel, or assisted by any member of the crew ? If so, was any payment made for this assistance?

9. OTHER INFORMATION : Other information (e.g. names and addresses of colleagues, community leader, e.g. mayor, tribal chief, contacts in other parts of the world);

10. STATEMENT MADE BY THE STOWAWAY :	**11. STATEMENT MADE BY THE MASTER :** Including any observations on the credibility of the information provided by the stowaway :

12. DATE OF THE INTERVIEW :	**13. STOWAWAY SIGNATURE AND DATE:**	**14. MASTER'S SIGNATURE AND DATE:**

that, after allowing the stowaway to be presented for examination and allowing your operator's representative to have access to the stowaway, they should give directions for the removal of the stowaway to the port of embarkation, country of nationality, or to some other country to which lawful directions may be made. Unfortunately, a number of countries, such as Japan, will not allow the person to be repatriated even if the country of origin has agreed to take the stowaway back.

This is what the Convention says should happen:

Taken from Article 4.13 of the Amendments to the Annex to the Convention on Facilitation of International Maritime Traffic 1965, as amended (Resolution FAL.7 (29))

4.9.1 The public authorities in the first scheduled port of call after discovery shall decide in accordance with national legislation whether the stowaway is admissible into that State.

4.9.2 The public authorities in the first scheduled port of call after discovery shall allow disembarkation of the stowaway if the stowaway is in possession of valid travel documents for return, and the authorities are satisfied that timely arrangements have been made or will be made and that all the requisites for transit have been fulfilled.

4.9.3 When appropriate and in accordance with national legislation, public authorities in the country of the ship's first scheduled port of call after discovery of a stowaway shall allow disembarkation of the stowaway when the public authorities are satisfied that they or the ship owner will obtain valid travel documents, make timely arrangements for the repatriation of the stowaway and fulfil all the requisites for transit. Public authorities shall, further, favourably consider allowing disembarkation of the stowaway when it is impracticable to remove the stowaway on the ship of arrival or other factors exist which would preclude removal on the ship. Such factors may include but are not limited to when:

(a) A case is unresolved at the time of sailing of the ship; or
(b) The presence of the stowaway onboard would endanger the safe operation of the ship, the health of the crew or the stowaway.

All of this hangs on the possession of valid travel documents. If the State the ship is in is assured that the travel documents are on their way and that they can repatriate the stowaway, then the ship will not be delayed as they can remove the stowaway to await deportation. An interesting clause is that of the stowaway endangering the ship himself or others. What if, for example, the stowaway threatens suicide if he cannot disembark? Or that he will kill the bosun when the ship sails? In such a case, the Master must notify the shore authorities and request the stowaway be taken off the ship. It will certainly help the case if the stowaway makes these statements in the presence of the shore authorities. At least have a witness to such statements and a record of your requests to have him removed because if you sail with him onboard and he carries out his threats, the first person the finger of blame will be pointed at will be the Master. I suggest that, if the authorities will not remove him even after such threats and you are ordered to sail by your operator, you make a statement of protest, ensuring you have a true log of all the events. You will also need to have him kept in a secure place and watched so that you can ensure his threats are not carried out.

5.2 The State of Embarkation

Taken from Article 4.13 of the Amendments to the Annex to the Convention on Facilitation of International Maritime Traffic 1965, as amended (Resolution FAL.7 (29))

> When it has been established to their satisfaction that stowaways have embarked a ship in a port in their State, public authorities shall accept for examination such stowaways being returned from their point of disembarkation having been found inadmissible there.

This sounds reasonable enough. But what if the stowaway is not a national of the State where he stowed away? They might not be so ready to accept him unless it can be proved that he really did embark there.

Because it could make it even more difficult to persuade a country that a stowaway boarded at their port once the ship has sailed, it is prudent in certain high risk ports to make a further search after sailing while the ship is still within the territorial limits. If a stowaway is found, return to the port to hand the person/s over. This is by far the cheapest option, especially as the Resolution states that there should be no costs or detention against the ship.

5.3 The Flag State

When any State refuses the disembarkation of a stowaway, the Flag State is to be immediately advised together with the reasons for the refusal.

Taken from Article 4.13 of the Amendments to the Annex to the Convention on Facilitation of International Maritime Traffic 1965, as amended (Resolution FAL.7 (29))

> The public authorities of the Flag State of the ship shall assist the Master and operator of the ship or the appropriate public authority at ports of call in:
>
> - Identifying the stowaway and determining their nationality;
> - Making representations to the relevant public authority to assist in the removal of the stowaway from the ship at the first available opportunity; and
> - Making arrangements for the removal and repatriation of the stowaway.

5.4 Inadequate Documentation

Most of the laws about the removal of a stowaway from a vessel depend on the stowaway having adequate documentation. In the event that such documentation is not available, there is provision for the State where the ship has arrived to issue a covering letter together with a photograph and other pertinent information. The State's willingness to issue the letter often depends on its own laws. As this letter is intended to authorise the return of the stowaway to either the country of origin or to the State/port where the stowaway began their journey, this State must also be willing to accept them.

Many of the ports will demand that a stowaway is guarded during the vessel's stay. In some cases, they will provide a security guard rota system that will be billed to your company. In others, they will take him ashore and imprison him until the ship is due to sail. As a final alternative, they might require the ship to guard him. Generally, you do not have facilities to hold someone securely and your crew are not trained as guards, so I strongly advise that you arrange for your agent to hire a security company for this purpose.

If you have to give medical treatment to the stowaway, get agreement to this in writing and/or on tape, in front of witnesses, before beginning treatment. When treatment or medication is given, ensure the stowaway understands what it is for and that the treatment is provided in front of witnesses.

Having a stowaway onboard is a complicated situation and you must remember that, regardless of the truth, the stowaway will often say what they think will assist them.

As an example of how wrong things can go:

In December 2005, a container vessel arrived in Belgium from Lagos with ten Nigerian stowaways onboard, hidden in the rudder stock area. They stated that two of their companions were missing and that they had jumped overboard. They later alleged that the missing two had been killed and thrown over the side, also claiming that the Captain knew they were onboard. The Master vehemently denied the allegations. He was eventually cleared of any wrongdoing in July 2006, seven months later.

In March 2007, the IMO's Facilitation Committee created a 'Stowaway Focal Point' (SFP) to assist Masters when other forms of assistance have not been successful.

1. The IMO Stowaway Focal Point will facilitate communications between the relevant Governments.
2. There will be a trial period of one year.
3. The SFP will be available during working hours (London time), defined as 09:00 to 17:30, Monday to Friday during the working days of IMO.

4. Member States, international organizations and non-governmental organizations in consultative status may seek the assistance of the SFP. However, the consent of the Flag State of the ship concerned will be required in the case of requests made by international organizations and non-governmental organizations.

5. The IMO SFP should be sent the relevant information contained in Form A.871 listed above.

6. The IMO assumes no liability.

7. There is no charge for using the SFP.

8. The primary function of the SFP is to provide assistance when the parties concerned have been unable to resolve such issues within the means available to them.

6 Port of Refuge

'MT Castor', Showing Extent of the Crack

> ***Place of Refuge***
>
> *A place where a ship in need of assistance can take action to enable it to stabilize its condition and reduce the hazards to navigation and to protect human life and the environment (IMO Res A.949).*

At the beginning of 2001, the fully laden 31,068 dwt tanker *'Castor'* developed a structural problem while in the Mediterranean. The ship suffered damage to the hull, resulting in a 24 m crack along her deck halfway along her length. Following the incident, the classification society (American Bureau of Shipping) withdrew the ship's certificates.

As the ship was thought to be in danger of a possible explosion or serious rupture of the hull, the authorities of Gibraltar and Morocco prohibited her entry into their waters or ports, effectively sealing the ship in the Mediterranean.

The ship then proceeded towards the coast of Spain, accompanied by a tug with which the owners had agreed a contract to trans-ship the cargo. However, the Spanish authorities, after inspection of the ship, described the situation as extremely serious with a high risk of explosion and recommended that the ship should not enter any Spanish port, but should instead be kept at a distance from their coastline. Any question of trans-shipment in Spanish waters was rejected as being a higher risk to the environment, population and coastal property than trans-shipment on the high seas. To ensure compliance, the Spanish government stationed several naval craft in the area. The Spanish Government rescued 26 crew from the ship and then ordered that the ship withdraw at least 30 miles from their coastline.

The salvors now towed the vessel to Algeria but again were refused entry, so eventually ended up off the coast of Tunisia where the cargo was safely unloaded.

The Spanish authorities had successfully completed their obligation under the SAR requirements and evacuated the crew. The Master's responsibilities for the safety of his crew also ended at that point.

Taken from IMO Resolution A.949 (23)

Guidelines on places of refuge for ships in need of assistance

1.18 A ship needing assistance means a ship in a situation, apart from one requiring rescue of persons onboard, that could give rise to loss of the vessel or an environmental or navigational hazard.

1.19 Place of Refuge means a place where a ship in need of assistance can take action to enable it to stabilize its condition and reduce the hazards to navigation and to protect human life and the environment.

3.1 Under international law, a coastal State may require the ship's captain or company to take appropriate action within a prescribed time limit with a view to halting a threat of danger. In the case of failure or urgency, the coastal State can exercise its authority in taking responsive action appropriate to the threat.

3.12 When permission to access a place of refuge is requested, there is no obligation for the *coastal State* to grant it, but the coastal State should weigh all the factors and risks in a balanced manner and give shelter whenever reasonably possible.

To assist Masters of ships in need of this assistance, States are required to have established an MAS (Maritime Assistance Service). This service is responsible for receiving all reports in the event of incidents and serving as a point of contact between the Master and the authorities of the State in the event of an incident.

In earlier times, ports recognised that they owed their existence to the ships and the seafarers on them so the 'port of refuge' was established as an international obligation to take ships in distress and provide assistance. Today you are quite likely to find a 'closed' sign on the door, especially if there is any danger of pollution. If you are really in distress and it is your opinion that you are endangering the lives of your ship's company if you proceed further, and they advise you that the port is closed to you, what are your alternatives?

The main aim is to protect the life of those onboard. If time allows then you will be calling for assistance from salvage tugs/helicopter and rescue services. But, meanwhile, the prudent Master should be closing with the nearest safe place, which will be land and a nearby port.

The guidelines offered by Resolution 949 in assessing the requirement for a port of refuge are:

Taken from IMO Resolution A.949 (23)

Guidelines on places of refuge for ships in need of assistance

1.13 The ship, according to the Master's assessment, is in need of assistance but not in a distress situation (about to sink, fire developing, etc) that requires the evacuation of those onboard; or

Those onboard have already been rescued, with the possible exception of those who have stayed onboard or have been placed onboard in an attempt to deal with the situation of the ship.

Should such situations then evolve to where the persons onboard find themselves in distress, the rules applying to rescue operations under the SAR Convention then have priority over any other guidelines for port of refuge.

With regard to charterers, if the deviation to a port of refuge is shown as being justifiable, then general average should be declared by the owner or the Master. Such justifiable deviations may include:

- Serious fire
- Structural damage, either from collision, weather or grounding that affects the seaworthiness of the ship
- Dangerous shift or leaks from the cargo
- Serious machinery breakdown
- Serious crew disturbance that threatens the prosecution of the voyage or the safety of those onboard.

Another reason could be shortage of fuel or water. However, general average would depend on the vessel proving that, when sailing from the previous port, there had been sufficient bunkers and water onboard for the voyage to be completed.

General Average

A legal principle of maritime law according to which all parties in a sea venture proportionally share any losses resulting from a voluntary sacrifice of part of the ship or cargo to save the whole in an emergency.

The onus is on the Master to make a good initial assessment. If he and the crew are not in immediate danger, ie not in a distress situation, but require assistance from a port to obtain either shelter or repair facilities to deal with a situation, then the port of refuge guidelines must be followed. Should the situation deteriorate, the Master is responsible for issuing a distress call and, in response to this, rescue operations under SAR will commence until the crew have been safely evacuated from the ship. Should a distress call be made, regardless of the operations already undertaken by others, the Master is still responsible for the safety of those onboard until they are clear of the ship and in a place of safety. Therefore, he must continue his efforts to ensure their safety until this occurs.

6.1 Towing and Salvage

Salvage Operation

Any act or activity undertaken to assist a vessel or any other property in danger in navigable waters or in any other waters whatsoever (Ref: International Conference on Salvage 1989).

The principles of salvage and salvage law have evolved over many centuries. They are based on the concept of encouragement of the salvor to effect salvage of the ship, property and life, and to prevent pollution. The encouragement is in the reward, which is based on even-handedness, enabling the salvor to share in the benefit to the owner of the salvage of the ship and the cargo, hence the term 'No Cure, No Pay'.

Anyone may salvage abandoned property but an owner who is still in possession of property may decline the offer of salvage. Marine salvage broadly involves assisting a vessel in distress, rescuing and towing a vessel at sea, assisting in overcoming fire or flooding or some other emergency assistance. If a vessel is in danger, any voluntary act meeting other requirements that contributes to ultimate rescue may qualify as an act of salvage.

6.2 Act of Voluntary Salvage

Voluntary act requirements may exclude salvage claims from those whose job it is to assist in salvage and the saving of life. This includes public employees, such as firemen, lifeboatmen or engineers employed for the purpose of salvage, the crew of the ship and passengers.

6.3 Towage

It is very important to clarify your position in the event of a breakdown where the ship and those onboard are in danger or if the ship is drifting in such a way that the incident could develop into an emergency. If you do require towing in proximity to land and, either through wind or current, are drifting towards land then a 'Safety' or 'Urgency' message will alert the authorities of that country to your situation. If there is time, the situation will be discussed with your operators. However, always remember all decisions are in your hands and that, regardless of their opinions or wishes, it remains your duty to safeguard the lives of those onboard. If this means that you need to call on assistance then this should always be done sooner rather than later. Bear in mind that Lloyd's open agreements can be made over the telephone or VHF if required. Should you be faced with a tug making outrageous demands, you will find in many countries there is legal provision for setting such agreements aside if they were made under duress.

The Lloyd's Standard Form of Salvage Agreement (LOF) originated in the 19th century and provides a mechanism for establishing any award due.

6.4 Tow or Salvage

To Salvage or not to Salvage...?

However, the big question is when is it a tow and when is it salvage?

In 2007, the *'Tramp'*, a small coastal vessel, departed from her berth in the river and got into difficulties trying to turn down river. Despite all efforts, the ship could not turn and in the end a small tug was called to assist the ship to bring her head around. The tug took a line from the ship and quickly brought the ship around. The task completed, the tug then let go and the ship proceeded down river. The tug then brought a claim for salvage based on the grounds that the ship was nearly aground!

Although this claim was rejected, the court concluded that the ship was sufficiently immobilised to found a salvage claim. Although the salvage service was small, it was successful and the ship was extracted from a difficult situation. The court awarded the tug £12,500 as opposed to the normal £625 tariff, not only as a reward for salvage but to encourage seafarers to provide such services.

This is an interesting award as I recollect the number of times that I have called for tug services in an emergency, especially when blowing off the berths in Hamburg and in Newcastle, Australia. Luckily, the tugs did not claim salvage! Equally, I have assisted a vessel in trouble in a Spanish port simply by taking a line as I was sailing by and assisting for a few minutes. I did not claim salvage. I think that the court is mistaken in the belief that we need encouragement to assist each other in such a situation, especially in a port or river, but then I am not a judge!

6.5 Pollution Compensation

In a number of cases, it may be that the salvage of a vessel or cargo will not be undertaken as the rewards are not worth taking on the task. However, the 1989 Convention allowed for a 'special compensation' (SCOPIC) to be paid that takes into account the saving of the environment from pollution.

Damage to the environment is defined within Lloyd's Open Form *as 'substantial physical damage to human health or to marine life or resources in coastal or inland waters or areas adjacent thereto, caused by pollution, contamination, fire, explosion or similar major incidents'*.

The compensation that may be awarded consists of the salvor's expenses plus up to 30% of these expenses if, owing to the salvor's efforts, environmental damage has been reduced or averted.

If a salvor has failed, through his negligence, to avert damage to the environment, his compensation will be affected proportionally.

7 Charterers and Charter Parties

A Charter Party is a written contract between the charterer and shipowner through which a ship is let or hired for the conveyance of goods on a specified voyage or period.

Libraries of books have been written about the legal ramifications of charter parties, and flocks of lawyers make their living from the disputes arising from them. It is important that you know the basics of the charter party and any clauses that are relevant to your ship as your role can severely affect the commercial success or failure of the owner.

The manner in which the obligations of the charter party are carried out in part depends upon the ability of the Master of the ship. The Master must ensure that everything required of the ship by the charter party is carried out in the way the charterer intends it. It is very strange that some companies fail to recognise this and don't provide sight of the charter party to the Master even though he is commercially obligated to follow it.

7.1 The Voyage Charter

A voyage charter is a contract of carriage to rent all or part of the cargo space of a vessel on one or a series of voyages. When a charterer contracts for only a portion of the cargo space, it is called a space charter.

7.2 The Time Charter

Under a time charter, the vessel is hired for a specific amount of time. The owner still manages the vessel but the charterer selects the ports of destination and controls the operation of the ship. It is a more permanent arrangement than the voyage charter and more representations have to be made about the ship to the charterer.

7.3 Bareboat Charters

This arrangement is completely different from the previous two. The charterer takes full control of the vessel along with the legal and financial responsibility for it, effectively acting as owner for the period of the charter.

7.4 Charter Party Disputes

The '*Count*' arrived at Beira and tendered notice of readiness on 29th June 2004. On the same day, another inbound vessel, *'British Enterprise'*, grounded in the channel linking port and sea. This vessel subsequently grounded a second time on 1st July. The *'Count'* proceeded to the discharge berth on 4th July and completed discharge on 9th July. However, the '*Count*' was unable to leave port due to a second vessel, '*Pongola*', having grounded in a similar position in the channel as the '*British Enterprise*', blocking the channel. The '*Count*' was not able to sail until 13th July.

Mr Justice Toulson, in the High Court, upheld the decision and reasoning of the tribunal in finding the port to be prospectively unsafe at the time of nomination. The Court accepted the view that the misalignment of buoys and the lack of effective monitoring did not constitute a temporary obstacle or hazard but rather a continuing risk to all vessels entering and leaving the port, including the '*Count*'.

The risk identified was such that it could not be avoided by good seamanship and navigation. In the circumstances, the delay caused to the vessel did not need to be of a 'frustrating duration' to render charterers in breach of the safe port warranty.

The judgment sets out some of the general principles of law relating to safe port warranties:

- A safe port clause obliges the charterer to nominate a port where, barring any unforeseeable future event, the characteristics of the port render it safe for the vessel at the time she will use it
- A port will also be considered safe if the vessel can arrive, use and leave without being exposed to any danger that cannot be avoided by good navigation and seamanship
- A port that would otherwise be considered safe must not be rendered unsafe by delay or hazard causing delay to the vessel unless it frustrates the charter itself
- Finally, nomination of an unsafe port is a breach of contract for which an owner may recover damages in respect of any loss through delay or avoidance, in accordance with ordinary principles of causation and remoteness.

An example of a safe berth dispute is provided in the case of the '*Carnival*' (1994), where the following judgment was made:

'If it is foreseeable that negligent navigation of a vessel may cause hull damage to another vessel, it is unnecessary to pinpoint foreseeability to the actual damage suffered. A berth may be unsafe having regard to the design of its fenders, notwithstanding the pilotage system and overall safety precautions at the port'.

7.5 Affreightment

Affreightment is the way a contract to carry cargo for a shipper is described. It is an agreement between the operator and the shipper either to carry goods or to give the shipper part or whole of the cargo space on the ship. The shipper pays the freight for this carriage.

Yes, She's a Fine Old Ship

Charterers rarely see the ship that they charter, if they did then some would probably not be chartered. Sometimes they commission a company to make an inspection for them, but generally they accept the ship on the basis that the ship's certificates are up-to-date and, if that is so, then the Flag State inspections and the ISM audit ensure that the ship is capable of carrying out their operational requirements.

7.6 Bill of Lading

The Bill of Lading (B/L) is a most important document as it is the title giving the holder 'right of possession'. It is evidence that the holder of the original document is the rightful owner of the goods.

The B/L is a receipt for goods that have been loaded into or onto the vessel. It is a document of title to the goods and a contract governing the receipt, carriage and delivery of the goods.

The reason that there is such a dispute over any endorsements to the B/L is that 'clean' B/Ls as opposed to 'dirty' are required by banks as a condition of issue of a Letter of Credit, the issue of which is a requirement for early payment to the exporter by the bank.

Important points when dealing with the B/L are:

- Check that the date of loading is correct
- Check that the cargo quantity or amount is correct
- Check that the cargo description is correct
- Check that the destination for the delivery of the goods is correct
- Ensure that any clause inserted in the mate's receipts is included in the B/L
- Check that the number and sequence of the B/L are correct and that all the original bills are signed
- If the bill is marked 'freight pre-paid', be careful as you do not have specific knowledge of this. This can only be signed on the authority of your owners/ operators or their agents
- You do not have to sign the B/L if it incorrectly states the amount or condition of the cargo (*'Boukadoura'* 1989). (See Mate's Receipt below.)
- You should not sign the B/L if it bears the wrong date (*'Almak'* 1985).

You may also refuse to sign if the B/L states that the port of discharge is not within the trading limits of the charter party or the port of discharge is an unsafe port ('*The Gazelle*', 128 US 474 1888).

You should not sign a B/L if you do not understand the language it is written in. It should be translated into a language you can understand or, if this cannot be done, then make out your own B/L.

All of this shows the importance of this document and the need to check what you are signing. If you have any doubt then you should refer to your owners/operators. Be careful if you are offered any letters of indemnity regarding discrepancies in the cargo quantity or condition. Such indemnities have no legal bearing and should not be accepted, no matter who tenders them.

7.7 Mate's Receipt

This is the receipt signed by the Mate responsible for cargo operations for goods received onboard the ship. It should be identical to the B/L.

This is now being replaced in many trades by the Standard Shipping Note.

This note or receipt should carry endorsements about the condition of the cargo, such as rust stained, pitting, broken bags etc. In addition, when there is a dispute over the quantity, the lower figure of the tally should be used and the number in dispute stated.

7.8 Deadfreight

This is a claim made by the charterer against the operator that the ship is not filled to its full capacity, although there can be a claim the other way. Examples of this claim might be that the ship did not load to her allowable marks or that too much ballast or bunkers were carried, both of which situations would limit the amount of cargo being carried.

7.9 Safe Port

An interesting judgment regarding safe ports was made in the case of the *'Eastern City'*, where Mr Justice Pearson said:

'Be it supposed that a port can be safe for a ship even though the ship may have to leave it when certain weather conditions are imminent, nevertheless such a port is not safe for the ship unless there is reasonable assurance that the imminence of such weather conditions will be recognised in time and that the ship will be able to leave the port safely.'

7.9.1 Safe Berth

A safe berth is a berth which, during the relevant period of time, a ship can reach, enter, remain at and depart from without, in the absence of some abnormal occurrence, being exposed to danger that cannot be avoided by good navigation and seamanship. When referring to the berth, the term 'Always Afloat' is a standard phrase in charter parties.

It is not uncommon for vessels, and particularly bulk carriers, to find themselves aground at low water when alongside to discharge a full cargo, especially in ports where there is no resident dredger. I specified bulk carriers as the cargo residue during discharge often falls between the ship and the berth, quickly building up on the seabed and forming a 'ledge' on which the ship's inboard side rests at low water. A quick sound around can quickly prove this to the port if the angle of the vessel at low water does not.

It doesn't always have to be the draught, as the following example of a safe berth dispute judgment in 1994 shows:

'A berth may be unsafe having regard to the design of its fenders notwithstanding the pilotage system and overall safety precautions at the port'.

If a charter party requires a vessel to go to a specific port but has no clause regarding its safety, then it is the responsibility of the operators to ensure that the vessel can enter, berth and leave that port in safety.

7.9.2 Qualified Safety Warranty

A standard charter party clause would state 'trading to be worldwide between safe ports, safe berths and anchorages and places' or similar. However, there are qualified warranties for safety and an example of such is in the 'Shelltime 3' form, which states:

> 'Charterers shall exercise due diligence to ensure that the vessel is only employed between and at safe ports, places, berths, docks, anchorages and submarine lines where she can also lie safely afloat, but notwithstanding anything contained in this or any other clause of this charter, Charterers shall not be deemed to warrant the safety of any port, place, berth, dock, anchorage or submarine line and shall be under no liability in respect thereof except for loss or damage caused by their failure to exercise due diligence as aforesaid ....'

In the event of such a warranty being in a charter party, it should, in practice, be regarded in the same way as a no safe port/berth warranty, as the translation of 'due diligence' can be quite liberal.

Regardless of safe port/berth warranties, the prudent Master will always ensure that the port and approaches to which his ship is ordered are safe for the navigation of his vessel, and that the berthing and subsequent departure can be safely carried out.

7.10 Laytime

Laytime is the period of time allowed for loading and discharging. A charter party may also be claused to provide separate laytime for discharging and loading.

7.11 Demurrage

Demurrage is the money payable to the owner for any delay in loading and/or discharging after the laytime has expired, the reasons for which the owner is not responsible.

7.12 Notice of Readiness (NOR)

This is notice to the charterer, shipper or receiver, or other person as required by the charter, that the ship has arrived at the port or berth and is ready to load/discharge. In most charter parties, the acceptance of an NOR is the date and time for the commencement of the laydays.

It is most important that this notice is tendered immediately the ship arrives, usually to the agent, who will then ensure delivery to the charterer. In many cases, the tendering of this notice is required during office hours, so there is urgency in delivery with a few minutes delay translating to a lost day or, in the case of a weekend, a wait until the Monday morning.

The standard way in which the NOR is tendered is usually by message to the agent, stating the following:

- The ship's name
- The date and time that the ship arrived within the port limits.

It will say 'The ship is ready in all respects to commence cargo operations in accordance with all terms, conditions and exceptions as per the charter party dated.............'

It is important that the agent acknowledges receipt of this NOR. If no receipt is received, send the NOR again until it is acknowledged.

7.13 On-Hire, Off-Hire

On-hire/off-hire surveys are usually carried out by independent surveyors, with the owner and charterer paying an equal cost for the survey. The on-hire survey will state the bunkers onboard (ROB), the general condition of the ship, the state of the holds or tanks and their suitability for the intended cargoes and any existing damage to the cargo spaces. Once this is completed, a delivery certificate that should be attached to the on-hire survey report will be issued.

The off-hire is similar, carried out at a time and place of re-delivery specified in the charter party. The charterer must deliver the vessel in 'the same good order as when delivered to the charterer, fair wear and tear excepted'.

A re-delivery certificate will be issued. Any repairs required to make good any damage can be carried out prior to delivery, after the re-delivery survey or they may have to wait until a suitable port or dry docking according to the agreed charter party clauses.

The charterer may be allowed to deliver the vessel 'dirty', with an agreed sum paid as compensation for damages.

Off-hire can occur during the period of the charter for a number of reasons and a charter party will normally contain clauses to this effect. They usually relate to the dry docking of the ship or to breakdown of the ship or cargo equipment, damage or accidents, or anything that prevents the normal operation to the charterer's requirements. In such an event, the charterer is not required to pay hire money for the duration of the breakdown. Therefore, off-hire can be specified as starting after a certain period and, on busy liner trades, it is not unusual to have the off-hire starting within a very short period. When ships are on such tight off-hire clauses, it is important that they keep a running record of any 'down time' and its reason.

At the end of the cargo operations, the ship's tally and that of the shore operations should agree.

Think of off-hire as having to fulfil three basic conditions:

- There must be a loss of time to the charterer
- The loss of time must be caused by an event that falls within the named clauses in the charter party
- It has the effect of preventing the full working of the vessel.

7.14 Cargo Stowage

The charter party wording should be checked for clauses regarding responsibility for stowage.

Are you responsible for stowage or are you supervising?

In the Canadian Transport Company v Court Line Ltd (1940) it was stated:

> *'The supervision of the stowage by the Captain is a matter of course, he has to in any event protect his ship from being made unseaworthy; and in other respects he no doubt has the right to interfere if he considers that the proposed stowage might impose a liability upon his owners. If it could be proved by the charterers that the bad stowage was caused only by the Captain's orders, and that their own proposed stowage would have caused no damage, that might enable them to escape liability'.*

The words 'under the supervision of the Captain' expressly give the Master the right to supervise the operations of the charterer in loading and stowing. It follows that, to the extent that the Master exercises supervision and limits the charterer's control over the stowage, the charterer's liabilities will be limited to the same degree.

If the charter party states 'supervision' and the Master limits himself to protecting the ship from damage and ensuring the seaworthiness of his vessel, then the charterer will be liable for any damage to the cargo.

I loaded a deck cargo of timber in Northern Canada for transportation to Europe. The ship was not a timber vessel and the cargo was loaded high with only chains securing the stow. I pointed out the inadequacy of this stowage to the charterer to no effect and, after discussions with my operator and because the ship would still be seaworthy, we sailed. In the Gulf of Mexico, the ship

encountered a storm and rolled heavily, resulting in the chains breaking and loss over the side of a good proportion of the cargo. On arrival at Cristobal, the cargo had to be restowed. All the loss and time delays were to the charterer's account as the Charter Party stated 'supervision'. I had also issued a letter of protest to the charterer holding them responsible for any damages to the ship.

If the word 'responsibility' is inserted in the charter party, the Master is responsible not only for damage to the cargo, but also to the ship.

7.15 Stevedore Damage

Stevedore damage on many ships is a way of life, especially at discharge ports on bulk carriers. Heavy grabs not only damage the hold but also impact on the steelwork in the tanks. Regardless of ship type, few Masters have not experienced some form of stevedore damage during their careers.

In most charter parties, the charterer is responsible for damage to the ship caused by actions of stevedores and/or their machinery. It is most important that any damage caused is brought to the immediate attention of the stevedores/charterers. It is recommended that photographs of the damage are taken and that all the relevant details are noted in the ship's log.

In the 'ASBATIME' Charter Party, the Stevedore Damage Clause states:

> Any damage by Stevedores during the currency of this charter shall be reported by the Captain to the charterers or their agents in writing, within 24 hours of the occurrence or as soon as possible thereafter. The Captain should use his best efforts to obtain written acknowledgement by responsible parties causing damage unless damage has been made good in the meantime.

The 'BALTIME' Charter Party also makes the charterer responsible for all damage caused to the vessel through improper or careless cargo operations.

7.16 Protest

There are two types of protest and these should not be confused.

7.16.1 Note Protest

This is a declaration made by a Master and notarised by a person legally authorised to do so. The Master declares that circumstances beyond his control have caused loss or damage to cargo or ship (or any other loss that might be subject to legal dispute). This protest may be extended for up to six months after the initial deposition. The original note should include the words 'reserving the right to extend the protest at a time and place convenient'.

The circumstances in which such a note might be tendered include:

- Loss or damage caused by weather
- Delays caused by weather
- Declaration of 'General Average'
- Breach of a charter party clause, such as sending the ship to an unsafe port
- Cargo condition.

When making a protest, all relevant documents or log extracts, together with witness statements, must be presented to the person authorised to take the deposition. The protest should be made within 24 hours of arrival at the port.

7.16.2 Letter of Protest

A letter of protest is a formal letter regarding any matter over which the Master of a ship feels that there might be a legal dispute or claim, holding the recipient responsible for any consequences of the matter being complained about. It is generally used in port. When making any such protest, a receipted copy should be retained on the ship and a copy sent to the operator.

The letter can be about many things, such as the cargo, the stevedores, the operation of equipment, the port, the berth and the Masters of other vessels. Should such a letter be received onboard from any source, holding the vessel responsible for any incident, this letter should only be signed *'for receipt only'*.

8 Insurance

Is all Insurance a Minefield?

In 1720, two companies were granted the monopoly to hull insurance, the Royal Exchange Assurance and the London Assurance. A small group of shipowners who were discontented with these companies operated in London, the most famous place of operation being Lloyd's Coffee House. These groups came together in mutual cooperation with other shipowners, insuring and being insured within the group. In this way, the basic P&I club concept was born.

In 1855, the first mutual protection society was formed and today they exist in the United Kingdom, the United States, Japan and Scandinavia. Over 90% of world shipping is entered into P&I clubs.

8.1 P&I Clubs

In general, P&I Clubs cover the losses arising from all incidents at sea, with the following exceptions:

- Hull damage
- Cancellation of contract and loss of hire
- Towage by the insured vessel or towage of an insured vessel
- Wilful misconduct
- Refugees.

This is a generalisation and there are other exceptions and inclusions offered by different P&I Clubs.

In the event of any incident, accident or injury, the following is the recommended course of action:

Always:

- Contact your P&I Club representative
- Call your owner or operator
- Investigate every allegation of injury or damage
- Collect evidence or documentation relating to the incident, including any defective equipment. Store it in a safe place and label the pieces of evidence. Throw nothing away
- Take photographs of any damage or circumstances relating to the incident
- Instruct witnesses to write a review of what they saw and heard, drawing a diagram if possible. This should be carried out as soon as possible after the incident. Write personal notes about the incident yourself.

Never:

- Allow a surveyor or lawyer onboard the ship or to interview crew members until he has identified himself and produced appropriate authorisation to satisfy you that he is acting for your owner or your P&I Club
- Allow surveyors or lawyers acting for the opposing parties onboard, unless you have authorisation to do so
- Give written material or physical evidence to opposing lawyers or surveyors. If in doubt, do not give anything to anyone or let anyone examine anything
- Give a personal opinion about who or what was responsible. Keep to the facts. If in doubt, say nothing
- Allow crew members to express opinions
- Admit liability, either verbally or in writing
- Sign a document that you know contains incorrect information. This includes making false entries in log books.

You can and should call Class, in addition to the P&I Club, at any time you suffer damage to the ship as any repairs will be subject to their recommendations. If repairs cannot be made at your present port, they can issue a temporary certificate of Class with a time limit, which will allow the ship to proceed to a port where the repair can be carried out.

A note of caution: I was involved in a case in the United States involving considerable time in court and a large sum of money. One evening, I came back late from shore and went to the bridge. There I found the opposition's advisors using torches to go through the ship's log books and papers. The moral of the story is to keep everything to do with the case, if not already ashore, locked up and secure.

8.2 General Average

This is a legal principle of maritime law in which all parties involved in a sea venture agree to share in any common loss resulting from a voluntary sacrifice of part of the cargo or ship to save the remainder. It goes back to the days when cargo was jettisoned over the side to prevent a ship from sinking. As no-one could decide whose cargo was to be thrown over, it saved any argument to agree to a shared common loss. The principle still holds good today.

General Average requires three elements that are clearly stated by Mr Justice Grier in Barnard v Adams (1850):

> *'1st. A common danger: a danger in which vessel, cargo and crew all participate; a danger imminent and apparently 'inevitable,' except by voluntarily incurring the loss of a portion of the whole to save the remainder'.*
>
> *'2nd. There must be a voluntary jettison, or casting away, of some portion of the joint concern for the purpose of avoiding this imminent peril, a transfer of the peril from the whole to a particular portion of the whole'.*
>
> *'3rd. This attempt to avoid the imminent common peril must be successful'.*

An example of this might be where there is a fire onboard, when to put the fire out it is necessary to flood a hold with water, damaging all the cargo in the hold irrespective of which cargo was on fire. The action was done to save the ship and the remainder of the cargo, so General Average would apply.

9 Ballast Water Management

With trade expanding and vessels getting bigger, the problem of invasive species has grown with devastating effect in many areas. The effects of the transfer of alien species in the seas were first recognised in 1903 in the North Sea, but it was not until the 1970s that the problem was first seriously considered.

In 1991, the first resolutions were adopted and in 1993 the IMO adopted a resolution for control of ballast waters. This lead to the IMO adopting Resolution A.868 (20) in 1993, 'The Guidelines for Control and Management of Ship's Ballast Water to Minimize the Transfer of Harmful Aquatic Organisms and Pathogens'.

Ballast water management plans and forms are now part of the ship's port entry documentation. However, as ballast water management is still a relatively new imposition on ships and their personnel, it is appropriate to quote a few of the relevant parts of IMO Resolution A.868 (20) that affect you.

IMO Resolution A.868 (20) states:

8.11 Where a Port State authority requires that specific ballast water procedures and/or treatment option(s) be undertaken, and due to weather, sea conditions or operational impracticability such action cannot be taken, the Master should report this fact to the port State authority as soon as possible and, where appropriate, prior to entering seas under its jurisdiction.

The above is most relevant in a situation where a port requires the ship to be completely de-ballasted, but by doing so the ship cannot be handled properly in a seaway. It also applies where a port requires the same and then expects the ship to anchor in winter conditions or in areas where high winds are prevalent.

9.1.2 Removing ballast sediment on a timely basis

Where practicable, routine cleaning of the ballast tank to remove sediments should be carried out in mid-ocean or under controlled arrangements in port or dry dock, in accordance with the provisions of the ship's ballast water management plan.

9.1.3 Avoiding unnecessary discharge of ballast water

If it is necessary to take on and discharge ballast water in the same port to facilitate safe cargo operations, care should be taken to avoid unnecessary discharge of ballast water that has been taken up in another port.

Notice the wording, 'where practical'. Who decides this, the ship? And if so, will the port accept the ship's decision?

9.2.1 Ballast water exchange

Near-coastal (including port and estuarine) organisms released in mid-ocean, and oceanic organisms released in coastal waters, do not generally survive.

When exchanging ballast at sea, guidance on safety aspects of ballast water exchange as set out in Appendix 2 should be taken into account. Furthermore, the following practices are recommended:

- where practicable, ships should conduct ballast exchange in deep water, in open ocean and as far as possible from shore. Where this is not possible, requirements developed within regional agreements may be in operation, particularly in areas within 200 nautical miles from shore. Consistent with 9.1.2 above, all of the ballast water should be discharged until suction is lost, and stripping pumps or eductors should be used if possible;
- where the flow-through method is employed in open ocean by pumping ballast water into the tank or hold and allowing the water to overflow, at least three times the tank volume should be pumped through the tank;
- where neither form of open ocean exchange is practicable, ballast exchange may be accepted by the Port State in designated areas; and
- other ballast exchange options approved by the Port State.

It would seem that, on the majority of bulk carriers and tankers, owing to the structural stress problems, the exchange method is the one most favoured.

9.2.2 Non-release or minimal release of ballast water

In cases where ballast exchange or other treatment options are not possible, ballast water may be retained in tanks or holds. Should this not be possible, the ship should only discharge the minimum essential amount of ballast water in accordance with Port States' contingency strategies.

This is not a 'get out of jail free card', but it recognises that, at times, it may not be possible to discharge the ballast water or part of it owing to weather, stability or stress on the structure. The following supports this case:

11.3 In all cases, a Port State authority should consider the overall effect of ballast water and sediment discharge procedures on the safety of ships and those onboard. Guidelines will be ineffective if compliance is dependent upon the acceptance of operational measures that put a ship or its crew at risk. Port States should not require any action of the Master which imperils the lives of seafarers or the safety of the ship.

If there is a good reason why discharge procedures have not been followed then you will be asked to prove your case. Log book records of the weather conditions and your stability calculations will be required to support your actions. The final two are worth noting:

11.10 When sampling for research or compliance monitoring, the Port State authority should give as much notice as possible to the ship that sampling will occur, to assist in planning staffing and operational resources.

11.11 The Master has a general obligation to provide reasonable assistance for the above monitoring which may include provision of officers or crew, provision of the ship's plans, records pertaining to ballast arrangements and details concerning the location of sampling points.

10 Operating in Ice

The dangers of sheet and pack ice in and around ports should not be underestimated, as the account of events affecting the *'MV Sussex Oak'*, approaching Hamburg via the River Elbe in January 1946, demonstrates.

'The vessel was held up in a narrow part of the river. The Master could not have turned round and gone back because the propeller or rudder would probably have been damaged by the ice or even have been lost. He could not go astern for the same reasons, and he could not anchor. If he had tried to remain where he was, he would have been carried towards Pagan Sand, and there would have been serious risk of the vessel stranding. If she had stranded, she would have been subjected to the risks ordinarily attendant on a vessel aground in a tidal river, and also to the risks of ice packing round the vessel and crushing her plating.'

Contractual Restrictions

There is a widespread practice of trying to restrict a vessel's trading activity to safe ports, within Institute Warranty Limits or other specific trading restrictions such as 'Great Lakes Trade only allowed between official opening and closing dates' (which in themselves will have the effect of restricting a vessel's movements to some ice-bound ports and areas). In recognition of the risk of damage to vessels and the incurred expenses, both the 1946 and 1993 NYPE and the Baltime form contain printed clauses that, despite the differing wordings, all restrict a charterer's right to order a vessel to (or remain in) ice-bound ports or areas and otherwise to force ice, giving the owner the right to leave a port on account of the presence of ice.

The broad effect of this type of clause is that it enables the Master to refuse to go to an ice-bound port and to refuse to face ice met on his voyage, without being guilty of any breach of charter and without prejudicing his owner's right to hire when he is waiting for proper orders or for a sea free of ice. The Master is also allowed to leave a port that is likely to become ice-bound, but is not obliged to do so.

An owner, in relying on these clauses when refusing an order from the charterer to proceed to a particular port, must establish either that the port is one where lights, lightships, marks and buoys are or are likely or about to be withdrawn by reason of ice or that the port is ice-bound. Ports that are naturally and ordinarily ice-bound, but which are kept open by icebreakers or other artificial means, are not ice-bound within this definition.

Buoy Stuck in Ice

Vessel Damage

Contact between a ship and ice can result in damage, particularly to the shell plating (as a result of crushing) and to the propeller (as a result of contact with ice during steaming). Consequently, disputes arise between owner and charterer about the responsibility for such damage.

Responsibility for the navigation of the vessel rests with the owner. As such, damage caused by ice (whether in the form of ice sheets, floes or bergs) in open seas during an ocean voyage will, ordinarily, be for the owner's account in circumstances where the charterer has legitimately ordered the vessel to proceed to a particular (ice-free) port.

However, following a recent House of Lords decision where it was held that charterers have the right to give orders on employment and navigation of a vessel, it is presently unclear to what extent, if any, a charterer will assume responsibility by way of indemnity for loss and damage sustained to a vessel (including ice damage) in circumstances where the charterer gives and the owner accepts specific orders about the route to be taken. In other words, to what extent will the navigation risk pass from owner to charterer? In the present context, it is suggested that the risk of collision with any obstruction en-route is a risk that will remain firmly with the owners. (See Ocean Routeing in the next chapter.)

An owner relying on specific ice clauses who elects to force ice instead of requesting alternative voyage instructions or waiting for icebreaker assistance to reach a port that the charterer has validly ordered the vessel to proceed to will not be in a position to make a recovery from the charterer for any damage to the vessel.

If a charterer expressly agrees (in the form of a rider clause to the charter party or by subsequent agreement) to provide icebreaker assistance to enable a vessel to reach and/or load and/or leave a particular port, in the absence of that assistance and in the event of damage to the vessel occurring as a result of forcing ice, the charterer will be liable for this damage unless it can be demonstrated that such damage would have occurred even with icebreaker assistance.

Further difficulties arise in circumstances where it is alleged that the Master's handling of the vessel amounts to a *'novus actus interveniens'* (new intervening act) and where icebreaker assistance is intermittent (for example as a result of a convoy of vessels serviced by a solitary icebreaker) and damage is sustained in waters containing ice from frozen packs as a result of 'humping'.

Damage sustained by reason of ice will be the responsibility of the charterer if the port or the approach to the port where the damage occurred is found to be unsafe because of the presence of ice. The '*MV Sussex Oak*', given her perilous situation during her approach to Hamburg, forced ice suffering damage as a result. It was found that the Master acted properly in so doing without icebreaker assistance and the charterers were held responsible for the damage on the ground that Hamburg was an unsafe port.

Effects of Ice Accretion

Consideration of the general principles relevant to determining the safety or otherwise of a particular port is beyond the scope of this book. However, with specific regard to ice and the danger it poses, a number of general principles apply:

(a) A port can be unsafe because of ice dangers encountered on its approach.

(b) The safe port regime with regard to ice is not changed by the existence of additional specific clauses dealing with remedies for ice dangers, despite subsequent comments from Lord Roskill casting doubt as to the correctness of this approach. The inclusion of such specific clauses is designed to provide extra protection for a shipowner against a known and identified peril. This cannot and should not derogate from the risk placed on the charterer for the safety of the ports to which a vessel is ordered.

(c) One of the factors in determining port safety will be the presence, or not, of icebreakers and their efficiency in keeping a port open to sea-going traffic.

(d) Additional specific clauses dealing with remedies for ice dangers may be of relevance in determining liability for vessel damage between owner and charterer.

It is worth looking also at the GENCON General Ice Clause, which states:

> In the event of the loading port being inaccessible by reason of ice when the vessel is ready to proceed from her last port or at any time during the vessel's voyage or arrival or in case frost sets in after the vessel's arrival, the Master for fear of being frozen in is at liberty to leave without cargo, and this charter party shall be null and void.
>
> If during loading, the Master for fear of the vessel being frozen in deems it advisable to leave, he has liberty to do so with what cargo he has onboard and to proceed to any other port or ports or the port of discharge.

Reproduced by kind permission of Julian Morgan of Morgans

11 Ocean Routeing

Your vessel could well be ocean routed, or you may be given the option of being ocean routed, because of the charterer's requirements.

In areas of the world where the weather reporting is poor or non-existent, in winter or hurricane seasons, or with ships that have a difficult task or cargo, I believe that ocean routeing has a place and can be a useful tool in the box, but not as a service to be used by all ships in all seasons.

Every mainstream time charter form contains a term under which the Master is under the orders of the charterer as to the employment of the ship, within the bounds of safety of his ship, crew and cargo.

But what about navigation? Is routeing a matter of employment or of navigation? To you and me, obviously navigation, but to others...?

In the recent case of the *'MV Hill Harmony'*, which was time chartered, the charter contained the usual employment clauses but no special routeing clauses. The time charterer, on the advice of the ocean routeing company, ordered the ship to proceed from Vancouver to Japan by the northerly, Great Circle route. The Master had experienced heavy weather on a similar voyage some months before. He disregarded the charterer's orders and insisted on taking the longer, southerly rhumb line route. The charterer claimed for the extra time and bunkers consumed.

The arbitrators held that the routeing instructions were 'employment' orders that the Master should have followed and that his refusal, based on his experience of the voyage some months before, was unjustified. Note the word refusal. How can you refuse advice only?

The owners appealed. Both the High Court and Court of Appeal found in the owners' favour but then the case was finally referred to the House of Lords. The highest English appeal court changed the decision of the High Court and the Court of Appeal and found in favour of the charterers.

The House of Lords ruled that an order for routeing is an employment order. Time charterers are therefore entitled to give routeing orders to the Master which, unless they compromise the safety of the ship, must be followed. In addition, it was held that the Master must follow the shortest and quickest route unless there are navigational reasons for not doing so.

From this we have the situation that the navigation of the ship and the safety of those onboard is still the Master's responsibility and he can take such action as he deems necessary to preserve that safety. The same applies to ports that he deems to be unsafe. The charterer cannot order a ship to take a route that is unsafe but who is now the judge of that safety?

Navigation is still the Master's responsibility. He is at liberty to change course for safety reasons. He can refuse to enter a port he considers to be unsafe and can, similarly, leave port if it becomes unsafe. The *'Hill Harmony'* decision does not alter these principles and neither does it give the time charterers the right to order the ship to take any route, however safe. The time charterers have the right to use the ship in a commercially advantageous way and can determine the route the ship takes, as a matter of employment. However, they cannot place the ship, her cargo and crew in danger.

I suggest that we, as Masters, are still responsible for the navigation and can deviate from the ocean routeing advice if employed by the charterers, but in that deviation we must show that their recommended route was unsafe and that we might have to get another opinion on that apart from our own.

The only advice I can offer on this is that, should you be under charterer's ocean routeing and you disagree with the recommendations, contact your operator and the charterer direct with your views and suggested options. If you believe that, by carrying on with the routeing directions you could be standing into danger, then you must tell them so and have a copy of your disagreement in writing or, at least, have witnesses to your statements.

12 Refugees

Refugees (Getty)

Taken from UNCLOS Article 12:

Every State shall require the master of a ship flying its flag, in so far as he can do so without serious danger to the ship, the crew or the passengers:

(a) to render assistance to any person found at sea in danger of being lost;
(b) to proceed with all possible speed to the rescue of persons in distress, if informed of their need of assistance, in so far as such action may reasonably be expected of him;
(c) after a collision, to render assistance to the other ship, its crew and its passengers and, where possible, to inform the other ship of the name of his own ship, its port of registry and the nearest port at which it will call.

1974 SOLAS Convention Chapter V Regulation 33, requires:

The Master of a ship which is in a position to be able to provide assistance, on receiving information from any source that persons are in distress at sea, is bound to proceed with all speed to their assistance, if possible informing them or the search and rescue service that the ship is doing so....

The above sets out, in no uncertain terms, the obligation of a Master of a ship to assist and rescue any persons in distress at sea.

The 1979 Search and Rescue (SAR) Convention obliges State Parties to:

2.1.10 '.....ensure that assistance be provided to any person in distress at sea. They shall do so regardless of the nationality or status of such a person or the circumstances in which that person is found'.

12.1 The Ship is not a Place of Safety

A place of safety is a location where rescue operations are considered to terminate and where:

- The survivor's safety or life is no longer threatened
- The basic human needs (such as food, shelter and medical needs) can be met
- Transport arrangements can be made for the survivor's next or final destination.

Resolution MSC.167(78) adopted in May 2004 by the Maritime Safety Committee

> The Government responsible for the SAR region in which survivors are recovered is responsible for providing a place of safety or ensuring that such a place of safety is provided.

The situation could not be clearer. The States that signed to the Law of the Sea, SOLAS and the Maritime Safety Convention are obliged to follow the above.

***'Tampa'* (Getty)**

The Norwegian merchant ship *'Tampa'* in August 2001, sailing from Perth, Australia under the command of Captain Arne Rinnan, received a call for assistance from the Rescue Coordination Centre of the Australian Maritime Safety Authority. The '*Tampa*' changed course and was guided by an Australian coastal search airplane to reach an Indonesian boat crowded with passengers and in acute distress. The boat was breaking up in heavy seas as the '*Tampa*' arrived, just in time to transfer the 433 people onboard to its own decks. The Norwegian ship had facilities onboard for only 50 people, including its crew of 27.

The closest port to the site of the rescue was Christmas Island, an Australian territory, but Australia's Immigration Department forbade the '*Tampa*' to enter

Australian territorial waters. The Australian government was determined to stop unauthorised arrivals of asylum seekers and so refused to disembark the '*Tampa's*' passengers and permit the vessel to proceed on its scheduled route. After long and tense negotiations, during which conditions onboard the '*Tampa*' reached crisis proportions, a complicated and costly arrangement saw the passengers forcibly removed from the ship and dispersed to camps in Nauru, a small State nearby. Some 132 refugees, including unaccompanied minors and families, were accepted by New Zealand, where almost all received refugee status. None went directly to Australia. In this long process, the owners and agents of the '*Tampa*' incurred substantial losses.

What often is not mentioned is that the Indonesian SAR service took over the rescue coordination and, after the rescue, ordered the ship to Indonesia. However, five male refugees invaded the bridge of the ship and aggressively ordered the Master to head for Australia saying 'they had nothing to lose', which sheds a different light on the attitude of the Australian Government. By law, when these refugees invaded the bridge and ordered the Master to change his course, their status changed from refugees to pirates. I have not yet heard of any charges being raised against those involved.

In the case of CA Venizolana v Bank Line Ltd 1988, the '*MV Roachbank*', on a voyage to Kaohsiung from Singapore, encountered Vietnamese 'boat people' in the China Sea. They were clearly in distress and, according to his obligations, the Master took them onboard. On arrival at Kaohsiung, the authorities refused permission for the refugees to land and the ship was kept waiting for nine days before berthing after the owners had provided suitable guarantees. The charterer tried to claim that the vessel was off-hire, but both the arbitrators and the Court of Appeal upheld that the ship remained on-hire.

In 2003, Norway put a new proposal for dealing with refugees to the IMO. Under Norway's proposal, should a country of asylum, even temporary, not immediately be found for the refugees, the ship's Master would have the automatic right to drop off his passengers in the country closest to the rescue point or in a country near the ship's planned route.

The 'docking' country would then be required to quickly shelter the refugees in a safe site or to make another boat available to transport them safely to another destination. Unfortunately, this was immediately opposed by the United States and Australia.

There is little more to say on the subject. We know our obligations and, apart from the clearly stated regulations, purely in the name of humanity we can do no less than stop our vessels and render all available assistance to anyone in distress on the seas, regardless of their status. We are not the arbitrators nor are we responsible for the reasons people are on the seas in such conditions. We have our duty and we must do it. We must however be aware of what happened on the '*Tampa*', and any ship taking onboard a large number of refugees and ordered to a place the refugees disagree with must be conscious of the possible reactions, especially when such reaction goes unpunished.

13 Mutiny

***'Columbia Eagle',* Last Act of Mutiny on a Merchant Vessel?**

Hopefully, the only time you will come across mutiny is when watching reruns of *'The Mutiny on the Bounty'*, but it is useful to know the definitions as, since the *'Bounty'* incident, it has become an emotive word that is too often used out of context.

The dictionary defines mutiny as 'open rebellion against constituted authority, especially rebellion of sailors against superior officers'. This is the military interpretation of the word and, because of this, there have been numerous incidents both ashore and afloat dealt with as mutiny or mutinous events.

Military law and common maritime law differ about mutiny at sea and its consequences. Mutiny, even on a commercial vessel during a time of conflict, especially when the commercial ship is engaged in military or support of military operations by nationals of the same nationality as the nation the vessel is supporting, can be dealt with under that nation's military law and those involved treated exactly as if they are in the armed forces of such country.

During peacetime, mutiny at sea occurs when one or more members of the crew unlawfully and with force, or by fraud or intimidation, usurp the command of a vessel from the Master or other lawful officer in command thereof, or deprives the Master of authority and command onboard, or resists or prevents the Master in the free and lawful exercise of the vessel, or transfers such authority and command to another not lawfully entitled.

Mutiny does not occur when insubordination, disobedience or violence against the Master is not accompanied by intent to remove the Master from command of the ship.

In other words, even if an act of violence occurred against the Master by crew members that effectively removed him from command, if the act of violence was not committed with the intention of removing him, there is no charge of mutiny.

It should also be said that, because of the seriousness of such a charge, both military and merchant officers are extremely careful to avoid even using the word mutiny unless there is no other way to proceed.

Even if the officers of a merchant ship should wish to level such a charge, there is no reason to believe that their marine administration would accept it.

There have been very few cases of mutiny at sea on merchant ships. Two famous examples are the mutiny that took place on Ferdinand Magellan's voyage and the mutiny on the *'Discovery'*, Henry Hudson's ship, when in 1611 he and his son with 11 others were abandoned in a small boat never to be seen again. The mutineers were never punished.

The last mutiny on a merchant ship occurred on 14th March 1970 when two American merchant marine sailors, Clyde McKay and Alvin Glatkowski, used guns they had smuggled aboard to take control of their ship, *'SS Columbia Eagle'*. The ship was sailing on a Department of Defence supply charter carrying napalm to the US Air Force bases in Thailand for use in the Vietnam war. This was the first armed mutiny aboard an American ship in 150 years. The Master was ordered to force 24 crew members into the ship's boats and the ship, with only 13 remaining onboard, sailed to Cambodia where the mutineers were given political asylum. Unfortunately for the mutineers, the regime in Cambodia changed and they were arrested. McKay escaped before he could be extradited but Glatkowski was returned to the United States and was charged with mutiny and assult, for which he received 10 years and 5 years respectively. McKay's remains, which were positively identified many years later, were found in Cambodia.

13.1 A Recent Act of Mutiny?

Consider again the case of the five refugees invading the bridge of the *'Tampa'*. By ordering the Master to take a course for Australia by threat of violence, they usurped the command of the ship, thus fulfilling the definition of mutiny.

However, they were not crew. If it could be argued that they did not commit mutiny, as they were not signed on the vessel as crew, then surely they committed an act of piracy?

The definition of piracy according to the Law of the Sea is as follows:

Taken from UNCLOS Article 101

Piracy consists of any of the following acts:

(a) any illegal acts of violence or detention, or any act of depredation, commited for private ends by the crew or the passengers of a private ship or a private aircraft, and directed:

(i) on the high seas, against another ship or aircraft or against persons or property onboard such ship or aircraft;

(ii) against a ship, aircraft, persons or property in a place outside the jurisdication of any State;

(b) any act of voluntary participation in the operation of a ship or of an aircraft with knowledge of facts making it a pirate ship or aircraft;

(c) any act of inciting or of intentionally facilitating an act described in subparagraph (a) or (b).

For the first time, we see the mention of passengers. It is recognised that piracy is a growing problem in lawless areas of the seas. However, in the case of refugees, we have a different situation. Now a vessel is obliged by law to take onboard persons of an unknown quantity but certainly desperate to escape from an existing predicament. In most cases, the vessel will have a small crew, often far less than those it is taking onboard, and will be unarmed. Once again, we have the Law of the Sea placing the Master in an invidious position. If his duty is above all else to the safety of his crew, could it be said that he endangered his crew by taking on refugees that subsequently committed violence against that crew to achieve their ends?

This is not to advocate that the Master should not assist such refugees, but all aspects of such a situation must always be carefully considered.

14 The Fair Treatment of Seafarers (After a Maritime Accident)

A photo taken on 2nd February 2000 shows Captain Krun Mathur of the *'Erika'* during a press conference in Paris. Mathur was placed under investigation for charges of 'marine pollution and endangering lives' and accused in the massive pollution of the French-Atlantic coast when the *'Erika'* sank in storms in December 1999. (Getty)

The IMO Resolution A.987 (24), adopted on 1st December 2005 concerns the fair treatment of seafarers in the event of a maritime accident. This Resolution:

Urges all States to respect the basic human rights of seafarers involved in maritime accidents;

Urges all States to expeditiously investigate maritime accidents to avoid any unfair treatment of seafarers;

Urges further all States to adopt procedures to allow the prompt repatriation or re-embarkation of seafarers following maritime accidents.

From this, there appears to be legal support for fair treatment of seafarers within the framework of international law.

In the Circular letter No. 2711 26th June 2006, sent to all member States by the IMO, headed *'Guidelines on Fair Treatment of Seafarers in the Event of a Maritime Accident'*, the following sections are of importance:

1. Seafarers are entitled to protection against coercion and intimidation from any source during or after any investigation into a maritime accident.
2. The investigation of a maritime accident should not prejudice the seafarer in terms of repatriation, lodgings, subsistence, payment of wages and other benefits and medical care. These should be provided at no cost to the seafarer by the shipowner, the detaining State or an appropriate State.

Under Section III, Guidelines for the port or coastal State, it goes on to state that:

9. The port or coastal State should:

   9.1 Take steps so that any investigation they conduct to determine the cause of a maritime accident that occurs within their jurisdiction is conducted in a fair and expeditious manner;

   9.2 Co-operate and communicate with all substantially interested States, shipowners, and seafarers, and take steps to provide seafarers' representative organizations in the port or coastal State with access to seafarers;

   9.3 Take steps to ensure that adequate measures are taken to preserve human rights of seafarers at all times, and the economic rights of detained seafarers;

   9.4 Ensure that seafarers are treated in a manner which preserves their basic human dignity at all times;

   9.5 Take steps to ensure/verify that adequate provisions are in place to provide for the subsistence of each detained seafarer including, as appropriate, wages, suitable accommodation, food and medical care;

   9.6 Ensure that due process protections are provided to all seafarers in a non-discriminatory manner;

   9.7 Ensure that seafarers are, where necessary, provided interpretation services, and are advised of their right to independent legal advice, are provided access to independent legal advice, are advised of their right not to incriminate themselves and their right to remain silent, and, in the case of seafarers who have been taken into custody, ensure that independent legal advice is provided;

   9.8 Ensure that involved seafarers are informed of the basis on which the investigation is being conducted (i.e. whether it is in accordance with the IMO Code for the Investigation of Marine Casualties and Incidents (Resolution A.849 (20) as amended by Resolution A.884 (21) or as subsequently amended), or pursuant to other national legal procedures);

9.9 Ensure that the obligations of the Vienna Convention on Consular Relations, including those relating to access, are promptly fulfilled and that the State(s) of the nationality of all seafarers concerned are notified of the status of such seafarers as required, and also allow access to the seafarers by consular officers of the Flag State;

9.10 Ensure that all seafarers detained are provided with the means to communicate privately with all of the following parties:

- family members
- welfare organizations
- the shipowner
- trade unions
- the Embassy or Consulate of the Flag State and of their country of residence or nationality
- legal representatives;

9.11 Use all available means to preserve evidence to minimize the continuing need for the physical presence of any seafarer;

9.12 Ensure decisions taken pursuant to the Protocol of 1978 relating to the International Convention for the Prevention of Pollution from Ships, 1973 (MARPOL 73/78) are consistent with the provisions of Annex 1 (Regulations for the prevention of pollution by oil), Regulation 11;

9.13 Promptly conduct interviews with seafarers, when done for a coastal State investigation following a maritime accident, taking into account their physical and mental condition resulting from the accident;

9.14 Take steps to ensure that seafarers, once interviewed or otherwise not required for a coastal State investigation following a maritime accident, are permitted to be re-embarked or repatriated without undue delay;

9.15 Consider non-custodial alternatives to pre-trial detention (including detention as witnesses), particularly where it is evident that the seafarer concerned is employed in a regular shipping service to the detaining port or coastal State;

9.16 Promptly conclude its investigation and, if necessary, charge seafarers suspected of criminal actions and ensure that due process protections are provided to all seafarers subsequent to any such charge;

9.17 Have in place procedures so that any damage, harm or loss incurred by the detained seafarer or by the shipowner, in relation to the detention of that particular seafarer, attributable to the wrongful, unreasonable or unjustified acts or omissions of the detaining port or coastal State are promptly and fully compensated;

9.18 Insofar as national laws allow, ensure that a process is available for posting a reasonable bond or other financial security to allow for release and repatriation of the detained seafarer pending resolution of any investigatory or judicial process;

9.19 Take steps to ensure that any court hearing, when seafarers are detained, takes place as expeditiously as possible;

9.20 Take steps to ensure decisions taken are consistent with generally applicable provisions of the law of the sea;

9.21 Take steps to respect the generally accepted provisions of international maritime law regarding the principle of exclusive Flag State jurisdiction in matters of collision or other incidents of navigation; and

9.22 Take steps to ensure that no discriminatory or retaliatory measures are taken against seafarers because of their participation during investigations.

Read Section 5 carefully. It does not say that the port State should pay for the seafarer's costs during detention, only that provisions are in place to ensure this. It could possibly be said that taking the seafarer to a bank would ensure that this was complied with. Guidelines 3 and 4 are equally ambiguous in their wording regarding the human rights.

Section 17 is also important for those at sea, but doesn't say, with regard to compensation, who should be responsible for payment. Once again, the wording is ambiguous. 'Having in place procedures' is not the same as 'shall compensate.' Without such a guideline, this is a ball that can be tossed around for years.

14.1 Flag State

The Flag State is also requested to follow certain guidelines from the IMO as follows:

10. The Flag State should:

10.1 Take steps to ensure that any investigation to determine the cause of a maritime accident is conducted in a fair and expeditious manner;

10.2 Assist in ensuring that shipowners honour obligations to seafarers involved in a maritime accident or any investigation;

10.3 Ensure/verify that adequate provisions are in place to provide for the subsistence of each detained seafarer, including, as appropriate, wages, suitable accommodation, food and medical care;

10.4 Assist seafarers to secure fair treatment, and assist shipowners in the event of an investigation by a port or coastal State;

10.5 Fund the repatriation of seafarers, where necessary, following the aftermath of a maritime accident in instances where shipowners fail to fulfil their responsibility to repatriate.

I do have the feeling that certain Flag States are not too interested in these obligations or, if they are, they lack the resources to fulfil them. Perhaps a proviso should be added that, if the Flag State is not in a position to fulfil these obligations, it will be necessary to appoint attorneys to act on the crew's behalf.

14.2 The Seafarer's State

Section V of the IMO's 'Guidelines on Fair Treatment of Seafarers in the Event of a Maritime Accident' concerns the seafarer's State and the following extract is of interest to us.

11. The seafarer's State should:

   11.1 Co-operate and communicate with all substantially interested States, shipowners, and seafarers, and take steps to provide seafarers' representative organizations with access to seafarers;

   11.2 Monitor the physical and mental well-being and treatment of seafarers of their nationality involved in a maritime accident, including any associated investigations;

   11.3 Fund the repatriation of their national seafarers, where necessary, following the aftermath of a maritime accident in instances where shipowners and the Flag State fail to fulfil their responsibility to repatriate;

   11.4 Assist, as provided for in national law, in the service of process and the return to a port or coastal State of seafarers subject to its jurisdiction who are needed solely as witnesses in any proceeding following a maritime accident;

   11.5 Take steps to ensure that its consular officers are permitted access to the involved seafarers;

   11.6 Take steps to provide support and assistance, to facilitate the fair treatment of nationals of the seafarer State and the expeditious handling of the investigation;

   11.7 Take steps to ensure that all funds remitted by shipowners, the detaining State, or any other State for detained seafarers, or for support of those seafarers' families, are delivered for the intended purposes;

   11.8 Take steps to ensure that no discriminatory or retaliatory measures are taken against seafarers because of their participation during investigations.

It must be noted that the seafarer's State is the State of which the seafarer is a citizen, by right of the passport that he is holding not his seafarer's documentation, which can be that of the Flag State of the ship.

One of the problems is that many ships are multi-national in manning, so there could be a dozen or so nationalities on the same ship. The question is whether any nation is going to follow the guidelines above for just one crew member? It would be far better for all the States involved to decide on one representative State acting with their authority.

The Flag State and the seafarer's State have both been told that they should fund the repatriation of seafarers. Unfortunately, this is a little like two people sitting in a restaurant and each leaving without paying, thinking that the other has done so!

14.3 The Shipowner

Section VI of the IMO's Guidelines deals with shipowners

12. With regard to investigations, shipowners have an overriding duty to protect the rights of the seafarers employed or engaged, including the right to avoid self-incrimination and to take steps to ensure their fair treatment, and should:

    12.1 Take all available measures to ensure that no discriminatory or retaliatory measures are taken against seafarers because of their participation during investigations and take steps to ensure that such conduct by other entities is not tolerated;

    12.2 Co-operate and communicate with all substantially interested States, other shipowners, as appropriate, and seafarers, and take steps to provide seafarers' representative organizations with access to seafarers;

    12.3 Take action to expedite the efforts of a port, coastal or Flag State investigation;

    12.4 Take steps to encourage seafarers and others under their employment, with due regard to any applicable rights, to co-operate with any investigation;

    12.5 Use all reasonable means to preserve evidence to minimize the continuing need for the physical presence of any seafarer;

    12.6 Fulfil their obligation in relation to the repatriation of, or take steps to re-embark, the seafarers; and

    12.7 Ensure/verify that adequate provisions are in place to provide for the subsistence of each seafarer, including, as appropriate, wages, suitable accommodation, food and medical care.

I think that some of these guidelines will come as a surprise to a number of owners and operators. It would seem that the shipowner is very limited in what he can do to ensure fair treatment and that no discriminatory measures are taken. With the best will in the world, these are the responsibility of Governments rather than private individuals. Guideline 7 is well within their abilities, especially as they will have an agent in the port.

It would seem that the seafarer is extremely dependant on the quality of the agent and his ability to deal with the port State, assuming he has fully accepted this responsibility.

14.4 The Seafarer

Section VII of the IMO's Guidelines deals with seafarers

13. Seafarers should:

    13.1 Take steps to ensure, if necessary, that they have appropriate interpretation services;

13.2 Take steps to ensure that they fully understand their right not to self-incriminate, and that they fully understand that when statements are made to port, coastal or Flag State investigators, these may potentially be used in a future criminal prosecution;

13.3 Take steps to ensure, if they consider it necessary, that they have arrangements for access to legal advice prior to deciding whether to give statements to port, coastal or Flag State investigators;

13.4 Participate in an investigation, to the extent possible, having regard to their right not to self-incriminate, with port, coastal or Flag State investigators, by providing truthful information to the best of their knowledge and belief.

It has been felt in many quarters that these terms are too narrow, as seafarers face contingencies other than those dependant on a 'maritime accident' when in port, coastal waters or even on the high seas, but to change them was neither practical nor prudent.

The Annex to the submission contains a list of principles that would apply for the protection of seafarers against detention following a maritime accident or incident or commercial dispute relating to their ship and/or her cargo.

Three of the principles have special relevance to seafarers:

- No seafarer shall be detained in the territory of any State beyond seven days from the date of the accident or incident or dispute alleged to have adverse consequences in that State [and] during the period when the seafarer is being prevented by the authorities to leave the country, he or she may only be confined onboard his/her ship provided it is safe to do, in appropriate accommodation and living conditions or in a hotel or guest house of comparable standards and from where the seafarer's freedom of movements is assured;
- The cost of accommodating the seafarer during the period referred to [above] shall be borne by the seafarer's employer;
- On expiry of the period [during which he/she is not allowed to leave the country] the seafarer shall be repatriated to the country whose passport he or she holds and into the personal care of that country's head of state, acting as agent of that state, and who will undertake to produce the seafarer at any subsequent legal or administrative proceedings in any country where the presence of the seafarer is required.

'MV Prestige' **(Getty)**

In 2002, the Master of the *'MV Prestige'* experienced catastrophic hull failure off the west coast of Spain. He requested port of refuge in Spain to shelter his ship and crew and discharge the cargo. This was refused. He then, as was his duty, ensured the safety of his crew by evacuating all but himself and two others onboard to support the salvage operation. The ship, owing to the continuing severe weather, broke in two and sank on 19th November.

This Master, who carried out his duties in an exemplary manner, saved his crew and continued to try to save his ship, was imprisoned by the Spanish authorities without trial and refused any legal aid or contact with any others who tried to assist him. Eventually, he was allowed back to Greece on a bond that he return for trial.

The *'Erika'* suffered a catastrophic hull failure in the Bay of Biscay in December 1999. The Master closed in on the French coast to abandon ship, which with the use of helicopters and a lifeboat he succeeded in doing with no loss of life before the vessel sank.

He was imprisoned for two weeks before being released to detention in Paris. He was eventually allowed to return to India in February 2000. This was another case where the Master did all he could and by his actions saved the life of his crew. In both of these cases, Class have not been called for trial and, in the *'Erika'* case, the Class society RINA placed the blame on the Master, even though the weather, at around force nine, was not excessive.

'Erika' **(Getty)**

It would seem that, apart from these cases and, with all the other arrests going on around the world, the fine words of the IMO have had little effect on maritime states who are imposing their own laws on seafarers as they think fit.

The latest legal fad involves cases where the operator of the ship goes bankrupt and abandons his ship. The Master, who will have suffered financial loss himself, is now 'detained' until he has settled all the bills on behalf of the bankrupted owner.

Case after case shows that, far from any desire to comply with the Law of the Sea, there is flagrant disregard for it and new national laws are being formulated that have the effect of further criminalising the seafarer.

Worse, the humanitarian aspect that we at least thought we could rely on is now in question. Take the case of the *'Delta Pride'* whose owner went bankrupt while the ship was in Mexico. The Mexicans confiscated the ship's documents and passports against a small supply of provisions.

With no owner and desperate, the Master sailed for Brownsville in Texas, hoping for proper legal proceedings to be followed. They were left without food and water for several weeks, existing on fish they caught and rainwater. The court in Brownsville sold the ship for less than it was worth. The internationally accepted procedures of the crew having first lien on the money were abandoned and instead they were taken into a detention centre and kept there for six months.

15 Shore Leave and Seafarers' Rights

The Conference of Contracting Governments to the SOLAS Convention met in London on 12th December 2002 and adopted Conference Resolution 11 on human element related aspects and shore leave for seafarers, which urged contracting Governments to take the human element, the need to afford special protection to seafarers and the critical need for shore leave into account when implementing the provisions of SOLAS Chapter X1-2 and the ISPS Code.

The following points are contained in the guidance to ensure this Resolution would be followed:

Shore Leave and Access to Ships Under the ISPS Code (IMO Circular 112)

There must be a proper balance between the needs of security, the protection of human rights of seafarers and port workers, and the requirement to maintain the safety and working efficiency of the ship by allowing access to ship support services such as the taking on of stores, repair and maintenance of essential equipment and other vital activities that are appropriately undertaken while moored at port facilities.

A port facility operator should ensure coordination of shore leave for ship personnel or crew change out as well as access through the port for visitors to the ship, including representatives for seafarers, welfare and labour organisations.

In addition to the above, the preamble to the ISPS Code clearly states:

That the Code must not be interpreted in a manner that is inconsistent with existing international instruments protecting the rights and freedoms of maritime and port workers.

To address these concerns and principles, Section A/16.3.15 of the ISPS Code provides that a port security plan must contain procedures for facilitating shore leave, crew changes and access for visitors. The guidance provided in paragraph B/16.8.14 reinforces this by providing that these procedures should relate to all security levels.

The case of Aguilar v Standard Oil Co of New Jersey, 318 US 724 (1943) included an analysis of policy reasons for the seafarer's right to shore leave. Excerpts from that decision include: *'Men cannot live for long cooped up aboard ship without substantial impairment of their efficiency. Relaxation beyond the confine of the ship is necessary if the work is to go on, more so that it may move smoothly. No Master would take a crew to sea if he could not grant shore leave, and no crew would be taken if it could never obtain it'.*

In short, shore leave is an elemental necessity in the sailing of ships, not merely a personal diversion. From this it is accepted that, in the US, shore leave is a right for crew under law.

In a visit to Fort Lauderdale recently, the port authorities completely ignored all of the above and prohibited the crew from leave, even to the extent of going on the jetty to get rid of garbage or visiting the seafarers' welfare centre within the port. The owner's agent actively supported this treatment.

At the ISF's Manning and Training Conference in London in October 2004, Efthimios Mitropoulos, Secretary-General of the International Maritime Organization, said in the keynote speech:

Governments and port authorities should treat seafarers as partners in the fight against terrorism and facilitate their access to ports and shore facilities. Fast turnaround times mean port stays are short these days and the pressure on seafarers is growing all the time. For the sake of safety and efficiency, as well as for the security aspect, they need adequate opportunity to relax and recover before they take their ships out to sea again in pursuit of their peaceful objectives in the service of world trade.

15.1 Seafarers' Rights Onboard

ILO Resolution 178 is partly based on ILO 147, the Merchant Shipping Minimum Standards Convention, all of which your Flag State should have ratified. It requires member States to implement a formal inspection system to inspect the following on their flag ships:

1. Maintenance and cleanliness of working and living areas
2. Minimum age of crew onboard
3. The Articles of agreement
4. Food and catering
5. Crew accommodation
6. Recruitment
7. Manning
8. Qualifications

9. Hours of work
10. Medical certificates
11. Prevention of occupational accidents
12. Medical care
13. Sickness and injury benefits
14. Social welfare
15. Repatriation
16. Terms and conditions of employment
17. The right to organise.

You can see where many of the above cross over into the scope of other inspections that occur on our ships and I am sure that many countries use other inspections to cover the points, but it does show that there is legislation that Flag States have agreed to ensure that their ships comply with certain standards. So why do many ships escape the net?

15.2 Legal Assistance for Seafarers

If you are serving on a ship and belong to a union or association, you will receive some form of legal assistance or advice in the event of any legal problem. If you are not receiving any assistance from your operating office, are not satisfied with any assistance received or there is good reason why you cannot receive such assistance, then it is from these unions that you should first seek assistance. Failing that, if your ship is ITF federated, the ITF should be contacted in any situation involving seafarers' rights.

In addition, every evening in the Stella Maris in Barcelona, which is a centre for seafarers' rights, a team of maritime lawyers meet to assist with legal questions for seafarers. Their telephone/fax number and email address are:

Tel: +34-93-4431965
Fax: +34-93-4431843
Email: apomar@icab.es

In New York, another centre for seafarers' rights produces booklets listing the legal rights seafarers are entitled to on various flagged vessels. The Flag States are:

- Bahamas
- Danish International Registry
- Cyprus
- Liberia
- Malta

- Norway
- Panama
- St Vincent and the Grenadines
- Filipino Sailors' Rights under Philippines Law.

The address from which to obtain any of these booklets is:

Center for Seafarers' Rights
241 Water Street
New York, New York 10038
USA
Tel: (212) 349-9090
Fax: (212) 349-8342
Email: csr@seamenschurch.org
Website: http://www.seamenschurch.org

16 Manning and Fatigue

Deadman Alarm or Snooze Button?

'Contracting Governments undertake, each for its national ships, to maintain, or, if it is necessary, to adopt, measures for the purpose of ensuring that, from the point of view of safety of life at sea, all ships shall be sufficiently and efficiently manned' IMO.

The regulations on Fatigue ILO 180, state:

Every seafarer must be provided with not less than 10 hours rest in total in any 24 hour period, provided that:

- The 10 hour period may be divided into not more than two periods one of which shall be not less than 6 hours; and
- The interval between consecutive periods of rest shall not exceed 14 hours; and
- The minimum hours of rest shall not be less than 77 hours in any 7 day period. However, STCW requires only 70 hours in any 7 day period.

On 25th November 1999, the IMO adopted Resolution A.890(21), The Principles of Safe Manning. It stated:

The minimum safe manning level of a ship should be established taking into account all relevant factors, including the following:

1. Size and type of ship
2. Number, size and type of main propulsion units and auxiliaries
3. Construction and equipment of the ship
4. Method of maintenance used
5. Cargo to be carried
6. Frequency of port calls, length and nature of voyages to be undertaken

7. Trading area(s), waters and operations in which the ship is involved
8. Extent to which training activities are conducted onboard
9. Applicable work hour limits and/or rest requirements.

The above is sensible and, if followed, should provide a good basis from which to ascertain the manning level. The Resolution goes on to list the functions on which the safe minimum manning levels should be based and include:

- Moor and unmoor the ship safely
- Maintain a safe navigational watch in accordance with the requirements of the STCW Code
- The number of qualified and other personnel required to meet peak workload situations and conditions, with due regard to the number of hours of shipboard duties and rest periods assigned to seafarers.

I consider the last point above to be a most important caveat to the manning considerations because, in almost every case, whenever the manning scale is questioned the word 'normal' is used. When any argument regarding the fact that a ship cannot perform its duties under duress is made, the answer seems always to be the same, 'but under normal conditions the ship can'.

The simple fact is that we have assumed a manning scale that on the vast majority of ships cannot cope safely and adequately with the peak workload situations and conditions that the IMO Resolution requires, and it has little regard for the hours and rest periods.

To further worsen the situation, in recent years we have seen a considerable influx of crews and officers of other nationalities with English as their second language. The MCA, commenting on SOLAS V, Ships Manning, states:

> English is to be used as the common language on the bridge of all SOLAS I ships unless a common working language has been established onboard and between ship and shore. The working language on the bridge of UK-flagged ships will normally be English. Under Section 51 of the Merchant Shipping Act 1995, UK ships may be detained if crew members cannot understand orders given in English and there are no arrangements for giving orders in a language which they understand.

MSC/Circ 1014 Annex Appendix 5, Section 6.7 states:

> The Company should ensure that the ship's personnel are able to communicate effectively in the execution of their duties related to the SMS.

Unfortunately, in many instances, rather than continuing with an attempted explanation to a crew member whose English is poor of how something is required to be done, it is often easier to use one of the remaining English speaking crew or just not have the job done. This compounds manning problems already existing.

IMO MSC/Circ 1014 Annex Appendix 7, Section 4.3.2 states:

> It is important that management recognises the potential problems stemming from the employment of multinational crews on the same vessels, a practice that might lead to language barriers and social, cultural and religious isolation, all of which may lead to safety problems.

It is impossible to separate fatigue from undermanning as the general fatigue on a ship is often directly caused by the manning problems. Regardless of the size of ship or its flag, the undermanning problem is universal in its effect. There is overwhelming evidence that fatigue is the cause of many accidents at sea and in port in addition to the general reduction in safety and additional accidents caused by undermanning.

It is important that the Master on any ship recognises the dangers that fatigue can pose in the very busy maritime environment. If fatigue is recognised and identified then immediate steps must be taken to alleviate this situation. If the Master feels that the manning of the ship is causing fatigue then he must bring this to the attention of the owners or operators. Equally, if there are language problems onboard that are, in his opinion, endangering the safe navigation of the ship or the operation of the machinery, then once again this must be brought to the attention of the operator. Operators of ships are often blamed for situations they have not been advised of in the first place.

As we all know, the records of hours worked are routinely falsified on many vessels, a problem affecting many ships of differing types and trades. The problem with this inaccurate record keeping is that, while accepting that the ships keep running and there is no disruption to their trading, should there be an accident and it can be shown in any enquiry that the Master falsified the records or knew of such falsification and permitted it, the consequences could be dire. I suggest that this is a point to think on.

17 Port State Control

Of all the inspections that we are involved in around the world, the Port State Control is probably the most practical as it is concerned with seeing the ship as it is. Unfortunately, many inspectors are tending to move from the practical aspect of what was intended towards a document checklist of the ISM system. This is a pity as we are already audited for that and a good safe seamanship type of check should always have a place in the checking of ships.

17.1 Areas Where the Port State Control Operates

When applied and coordinated on a regional basis, PSC is considered an effective and proven method of ship inspection. The following regional PSC agreements are currently in operation:

- Paris Memorandum of Understanding (PMoU) on Port State Control adopted in Paris in 1982;
- Acuerdo de Viña del Mar (Viña del Mar or Latin-America Agreement), signed in Viña del Mar (Chile) in 1992;
- Memorandum of Understanding on Port State Control in the Asia-Pacific Region (TMoU), signed in Tokyo in 1993;
- Memorandum of Understanding on Port State Control in the Caribbean Region (Caribbean MoU) signed in Christchurch, Barbados in 1996;
- Memorandum of Understanding on Port State Control in the Mediterranean Region (Mediterranean MoU), signed in Malta in 1997;
- Indian Ocean Memorandum of Understanding on Port State Control (Indian Ocean MoU) signed in Pretoria, South Africa on 5th June 1998;
- Memorandum of Understanding for the West and Central African Region (Abuja MoU) signed in Abuja, Nigeria in 1999;

- Memorandum of Understanding on Port State Control in the Black Sea signed in Istanbul, Turkey in 2000; and
- Arab States of the Gulf (Riyadh MoU), signed in Riyadh in 2004.

The United States does not have a regional agreement and carries out PSC on a unilateral basis.

The current membership is 27 maritime authorities made up of 22 EU countries and 5 non-EU countries covering some 600 ports.

17.2 The Inspectors

PSCOs (Port State Control Officers) should be qualified as a Master or chief engineer and have appropriate seagoing experience or have maritime related qualifications from an institution recognised by the administration, typically naval architect or mechanical engineer. They will be provided with specialised training to ensure adequate competence and skills.

17.3 Targeting Ships

Inspections within the PMoU region are targeted at vessels of most concern or those most likely to be substandard based on current risk assessment factors. The Black, Grey, White system is based on 3 year rolling detention records of Flag States with minimum number of inspections within the PMoU and is not affected by the number of deficiencies to a ship. It is updated to 31st December of each year and released in May of the next year.

The criteria for targeting include:

- Black flag listed ships have 4 risk levels that vary from medium to very high risk. They are given from 4 points to 20 points;
- Certain types of ships for expanded inspection are given 5 points;
- Age of ship above 13 years, depending on the age band, are given 1 to 3 points;
- Non-EU recognised Classification Society given 3 points;
- Flag States who have not ratified main conventions are given 1 point;
- Targeted Flag States above the excess of average will be given 1 to 3 points;
- Entering the region for the first time in the last 12 months will be given 20 points;
- Not inspected in the last 6 months will be given 10 points;

- Ship detained will be given 15 points;
- Number of deficiencies varies from 0 deficiencies given minus 15 points, 1 to 2 deficiencies given 0 points, 6 to 10 deficiencies given 5 points, 11 to 20 given 10 points and 21 plus deficiencies given 15 points;
- Outstanding deficiencies from last inspection for 'rectify before departure' or 'rectify at next port' are given 1 point and where noted 'all deficiencies rectified' minus 2 points.

17.4 The White List

The White List represents quality flags with a consistently low detention record. France, Bermuda and China are currently placed highest in terms of performance. The 2007 White List included 38 Flag States.

17.5 The Grey List

23 Flag States with an average compliance were on the Grey List in 2007.

17.6 The Black List

The PMoU Black List contained 19 Flag States in 2007. The poorest performing flags of the 19 Flag States on the PMoU Black List were Democratic People's Republic of Korea (NK), Bolivia and Albania.

A flag's ranking on the Black List is taken into account when targeting ships for inspection and ships with flags on the Black List are liable to a 'more detailed inspection'.

17.7 Inspections

You can see that entering a port for the first time in any PMoU region on a 30 year old bulk carrier flying the Albanian flag will generally cause some interest in the local official community and lead to a procession up the gangway relatively quickly.

Over a 3 year period 2005-2007, there were 65,745 inspections and 3,418 detentions. For those 3 consecutive years, the number of detentions increased from 944 in 2005 to 1,174 in 2006 and 1,250 in 2007.

- Ships flying a Black Listed flag had the highest detention rate of 11.62%
- Ships flying a Grey Listed flag had a detention rate of 6.49%
- Ships flying a White Listed flag had a rate of 2.88%.

In 2007, 12 ships that were flying a Black Listed flag due to multiple detentions, jumping detention or a ship not proceeding to the agreed repair port following detention were banned from the PMoU region.

In 2007, there was an increase in certain areas of deficiencies compared with 2006:

- Certification of crew (15.4%)
- Safety (6.5%)
- Security (5.4%)
- Marine pollution and environment (13.9%)
- Working and living conditions (16.3%)
- Operational (19.2%)
- Management (50.9%).

17.8 Types of Inspections

1. **Initial Inspection** which consists of a visit onboard a ship to check the validity of certificates and other documents and the overall condition of the ship, its equipment and crew.
2. **More Detailed Inspection** which is conducted where there are 'clear grounds'. Clear grounds are established where there is evidence that the ship's equipment or its crew do not correspond substantially with the requirement of the relevant conventions or that the Master or crew members are not familiar with essential shipboard procedures relating to safety of ships or the prevention of pollution. PSC will then:
   - Conduct a more detailed inspection in the area(s) where clear grounds were established
   - Carry out a more detailed inspection in other areas at random
   - Further check compliance with onboard operational requirements (operational control such as emergency drills and demonstration of training in use of equipment by personnel as opposed to just functional tests or checks).

   Ports have additional criteria for 'clear grounds' that may be identified before boarding a ship for inspection, for example Black Listed flag ships, flags that have not ratified the relevant instruments, certain outstanding deficiencies from last inspection and reported ships that become an overriding priority when a complaint is received from a bone fide source.

3. **Mandatory Expanded Inspection (MEI).** This is required at intervals of not less than 12 months to certain types of ships with a target factor of 12 and over, such as:
   - Oil tankers above 3000 GT and over 15 years of age
   - Bulk carriers over 12 years old
   - Passenger ships over 15 years old
   - Gas and chemical tankers over 10 years old.

17.9 Detention

I have mentioned the growing importance of ISM within the port state inspection regime. Depending on the seriousness of the case, the areas that may warrant detention by PSC are:

- ISM certificates not onboard
- Company on the DOC not the same as on the SMC
- Safety management documentation not onboard
- Relevant safety information not in a working language or language understood by the crew
- Senior officers unable to identify operator and DP (*DP does not have to be directly contactable*)
- No procedures to contact the company in emergency situations
- Drills have not been carried out according to the programme
- New crew members are not familiar with their duties in the SMS
- Master's overriding authority not documented and unaware of their authority
- No records of maintenance kept or no evidence of maintenance being carried out as indicated in the records.

17.10 Safeguards

What can you do if you wish to protest the findings of a Port State Control Officer? Not really very much is the answer. The first protest is made to the Port State making the inspection, but when a dispute cannot be resolved with a Port State within the PMoU region they may submit their case for review. The Review Panel comprises representatives, on a rotating basis, from four different PMoU Authorities and the PMoU Secretariat. Within the legislation of each PSC, there should also be a means for legal appeal through the courts or another form such as arbitration. I am sure that the time involved in such procedures can be imagined which is probably why so few ships or companies use this, and instead just accept their medicine.

18 The Law in Inland Waters

During the course of a voyage, a number of countries will be visited and the Government and laws of these states will vary, quite dramatically on occasion. The differences between Flag State and Port State causes a problem. The Master is expected to manage the ship under the law of the Flag State and, in that law, no Flag State differentiates between being in another country's sovereign territory or on the seas. However, the Sovereign State also expects its laws to be followed.

The commercial ship, unlike the warship or government ship, has no sovereign rights while within the inland waters of a State. This means that the laws of the Port State must be adhered to and, where the Flag State and Port State differ, the supremacy of domestic jurisdiction will take precedence.

The problem for the ship is that, in most cases, the Master has no knowledge of the laws of the Port State so the rights of the ship and/or those onboard can be violated through ignorance. An example would be police boarding the ship and demanding to search the vessel with no search warrant. Only they know if such a warrant is required by their law. Even in the UK, searches have been carried out on ships without such a warrant because the Master's ignorance of the law prevented him asking to see it. It must be said that there are as many cases of ignorance of the law extending to public officials as there is an understanding about how to deal with foreign flag vessels.

While the public officials of the Port State have right of access to the ship, only the laws of the Port State will decree the rights they have while onboard.

Non-public officials do not have any such rights and their presence onboard is one of sufferance by the ship. The Master may at any time request their departure. Should someone be onboard a vessel without permission, it is trespass and they can be ordered to leave or, in extreme circumstances, they may be removed. In this last act, care must be taken about Port State laws and it is wise, rather than having ship's personnel taking action, that the Port State authorities be called and requested to carry out the removal.

Private security personnel have no more rights than ordinary citizens when boarding a visiting vessel. However, when ashore in the port, all the ship's personnel must follow not just the laws of the State, but also the local requirements of the port or terminal itself.

As always, in any serious situation or if it is thought that such a situation could develop, advice must be sought from your operating office or, failing that, from agents or local legal advisors. Advice can also be obtained from the Flag State consulate or embassy. In the event of crew being involved in any serious dispute with the shore authorities, their national consulate or embassy should be informed as well as that of the Flag State.

18.1 The Arrest of Ships

A maritime claim can arise out of one or more of the following:

- Loss or damage caused by the operation of the ship
- Loss of life or personal injury occurring, whether on land or on water, in direct connection with the operation of the ship
- Salvage operations or any salvage agreement including, if applicable, special compensation relating to salvage operations in respect of a ship that, by itself or its cargo, threatens damage to the environment
- Damage or threat of damage caused by the ship to the environment
- Costs or expenses relating to the raising, removal, recovery, destruction or the rendering harmless of a ship that is sunk, wrecked, stranded or abandoned, including anything that is or has been aboard such a ship, and costs or expenses relating to the preservation of an abandoned ship and maintenance of its crew
- Any agreement relating to the use or hire of the ship, whether contained in a charter party or otherwise
- Any agreement relating to the carriage of goods or passengers onboard the ship, whether contained in a charter party or otherwise
- Loss of or damage to goods (including luggage) carried onboard the ship
- General Average

- Towage
- Pilotage
- Goods, materials, provisions, bunkers, equipment (including containers) supplied or services rendered to the ship for its operation, management, preservation or maintenance
- Construction, reconstruction, repair, converting or equipping of the ship
- Port, canal, dock, harbour and other waterway dues and charges
- Wages and other sums due to the Master, officers and other members of the ship's complement in respect of their employment on the ship, including costs of repatriation and social insurance contributions payable on their behalf
- Disbursements incurred on behalf of the ship or its owners
- Insurance premiums (including mutual insurance calls) in respect of the ship, payable by or on behalf of the shipowner or demise charterer
- Any commissions, brokerage or agency fees payable in respect of the ship, by or on behalf of the shipowner or demise charterer
- Any dispute as to ownership or possession of the ship
- Any dispute between the co-owners of the ship as to the employment or earnings of the ship
- A mortgage or charge of the same nature as the ship
- Any dispute arising out of the contract for the sale of the ship.

18.2 The Powers of Arrest

Two important clauses regarding the powers of arrest are:

- ***A ship may be arrested or released from arrest only under the authority of a court of the State party in which the arrest is effected***
- ***A ship may only be arrested in respect of a maritime claim.***

It should be noted that in the Arabian Gulf State's maritime codes and laws there are no provisions defining wrongful arrest or detention, neither are these acts prohibited by any conditions. This has led to a situation where agents and other parties, such as chandlers, have used their influence to have ships detained.

18.3 Release from Arrest

A ship that has been arrested will be released when sufficient security has been provided in a satisfactory form, save in cases where a ship has been arrested in respect of maritime claims regarding dispute of ownership or possession of the ship or any dispute between the co-owners of the ship about the employment or earnings of the ship. In such cases, the court may permit the person in possession of the ship to continue trading after providing sufficient security.

18.4 The ISPS Code

The ISPS Code provides an international framework through which the States, ports and ships can together co-operate to detect and deter threats to their security. It is designed to manage the risk element while providing an exchange of information between all the concerned parties to assist with evaluation of the risk and the containment of the same.

The requirements for ships and their owners are:

- Ship security plans
- Ship security officers
- Company security officers
- Certain onboard equipment.

The ports must provide:

- Port facility security plans
- Port facility security officers.

In addition, the requirements for both ports and ships are:

- Monitoring and controlled access
- Monitoring the activity of people and cargo
- Ensuring that the security communications are readily available.

The responsibility of the security officer and the mandatory drills are clearly defined within the Code.

If there is any reason to suspect that the security of the ship or port has been compromised, the ship may be subject to further control measures. These could include providing information regarding the ship, cargo, passengers and crew.

There is provision for denying the vessel entry to a port should it be suspected that the security of the ship, or the port it previously visited, or any other ship with which it may have interfaced, has been in violation of the Code.

19 Conclusion

The Law is not Written in Tablets of Stone

As you progress through your career at sea, you will realise that the law, especially international maritime law, is not written on tablets of stone. It is often written in hope rather than as a decree. While speedy to take disciplinary action against those at sea, it is far less speedy when taking action against those authorities and signatory states who disregard the laws. Many of the laws start as good, well meaning and well intentioned, only to appear at the end of all the debates and conferences as a very different and watered down version of the original intent.

The law is also ambiguous, often deliberately so, owing to the political nature of many international agreements. This ambiguity allows for too many interpretations, which guarantee the need for lawyers to find their way through the maze. This can be so complex that, in most cases, arbitration or agreements will be reached by the parties involved rather than going to judgment. You could well find that, while you may be involved in such arbitration, it is relatively rare that you will find yourself involved in a full Admiralty court trial.

We require and expect clarity where it does not always exist. Instead, we must make do with what is in place and learn to work with it. With this in mind, do not expect too much of the law, but understand what does exist and learn to work within its framework.

At the present time, regardless of where we are from or the flag our ship flies, the countries we are sailing between, or the actions and support of our owners or operators and the unions or associations to which we belong, there seems to be very little our own governments are doing about the arrests and detentions. If we are working for a ship management company or an owner who is a name plate on some island hideaway, that leaves only the unions. If you do not belong to a Masters' association or union, as many Masters do not, then you could well be on your own.

The International Federation of Shipmasters' Associations continues to work hard on behalf of Shipmasters worldwide and they have made a particular issue of the criminalisation of seafarers.

Even for those who have support, it can be a harrowing experience, with the possibility of receiving a criminal record for something that was absolutely nothing to do with you.

The ratification of the IMO Resolution on the Fair Treatment of Seafarers will assist considerably in dealing with many of the legal problems we can encounter but, even then, it is entirely dependant on the willingness of the Flag States to follow the laws and regulations. Unfortunately, this Resolution still does not deal with the civil problems stemming from the differences between the Flag State and Port State and the protection of the civil rights of seafarers in port.

The Master of an international ship, with his multi-national crew, is required to follow and comply with so many separate regulations. There is the Law of the Sea, then the laws of his Flag State, then the laws of the Port State whose waters he is in. Without doubt, there is sometimes conflict between these laws, and when this occurs he has to determine which have precedence or, as too often happens, which authority is holding the gun at the time.

With regard to Flag States, many do not bother to ensure that copies of their laws that the Master must follow are even onboard the ship. I certainly never had a copy of the laws of Liberia or Panama, nor on any inspection or survey were these required to be sighted.

Over and above your duty to follow the Law of the Sea, the laws of the Flag State, the laws of the States whose waters you pass through and the laws of the States whose inland waters you enter, your duty to the safety of your crew remains your highest priority. This must take precedence over everything, even when other laws might conflict with the actions or decisions made in pursuit of this obligation.

In the unfortunate event that you are involved in any casualty, you must remember that all communications and documents generated after the incident will normally be subject to disclosure to the other party. There is a privileged communication, which is recognised in the UK and many other countries, that is prepared at the request of your or the owner's lawyers for the sole purpose of subsequent litigation. Such communication is then privileged communication between your lawyer and yourself and not subject to disclosure. Before bursting into print, emailing or faxing any communication, check with your owners first.

As Master, you are not Expected to Know all of the Laws you will Come Across

No Master can hope to fully know or understand the maze of laws that he will encounter during his time in command. It is therefore essential that your operating office recognises its responsibilities in providing assistance and guidance, either directly or through its agents. Government representatives, consulates and embassies tend to listen more carefully to the chief executives of shipping companies than they do to a Master of a ship. It is essential that you have confidence that such support will be available should it be required.

I have often heard complaints from lawyers, P&I Club assessors and ship operators that many problems are caused by Masters not knowing or following the laws. The problem is that the laws are not written for us. Any seafarer who has ever had the misfortune to attend an Admiralty court or marine arbitration is often bewildered by two things. One is the fact that those sitting in judgment have little or no experience of what they are judging on, and two that this does not matter as they are only interested in the academics of the law rather than the justice or fairness of the case. Whatever the circumstances of your attendance, you will generally emerge bruised and more uncertain than when you went in.

Be certain that the standard rule of law around the world will apply, and the smaller you are, the more you will have to comply and as a Master of a ship in a foreign port in a foreign country wearing a foreign flag, you are small indeed!